MASTERY 500 AI Prompts for Business Success

MASTERY
500 AI Prompts
for Business
Success

ChatGPT Business Prompts to Drive Growth, Optimize Strategy, Boost Sales, Enhance Leadership and Innovate with AI

Mindscape Artwork Publishing

Mauricio Vasquez

Toronto, Canada

Authors: Mauricio Vasquez

First Printing: March 2025

978-1-998729-15-9 (Paperback)
978-1-998729-14-2 (Hardcover book)
978-1-998729-13-5 (Electronic book)

Scan the QR code to access our book collection.

Get Your Free Digital Copy

As a valued reader, I want to ensure you get the most out of this book in a way that's convenient and accessible. That's why I'm offering you a **FREE electronic copy** of this book!

Having a digital version allows you to:

(1) **Easily search and reference specific prompts** anytime, anywhere.

(2) **Access your AI-powered business insights on the go** from your smartphone, tablet, or computer.

(3) **Copy and paste prompts directly into ChatGPT** for faster implementation.

To get your free digital copy, simply scan the QR code below!

Table of Contents

Chapter 1 9

INTRODUCTION 9

Chapter 2 10

WHAT IS GENERATIVE ARTIFICIAL INTELLIGENCE? 10

Chapter 3 11

WHAT ARE NATURAL LANGUAGE PROCESSING CHATBOTS? 11

Chapter 4 11

BENEFITS OF USING CHATGPT 11

Chapter 5 13

WHAT ARE PROMPTS? 13

Chapter 6 13

FOUNDATIONAL PRINCIPLES FOR USING CHATGPT 13

Chapter 7 15

BEST PRACTICES TO MASTER PROMPTS..15

Chapter 8 46

BUSINESS PROMPTS 46

A. Business Strategy & Planning...46

B. Marketing & Brand Development 51

C. Sales & Revenue Growth 57

D. Product Development & Innovation 63

F. Operations & Process Optimization 72

G. Financial Management & Investment..76

H. Human Resources & Team Development..82

I.   Leadership & Management 85

J. Digital Transformation & Technology 89

K. Data Analysis & Business Intelligence 93

L. Market Research & Competitive Analysis 95

M. Content Creation & Communication 97

N. Project Management 99

O. Legal & Compliance 102

P. Risk Management & Crisis Handling..104

R. Sustainability & Corporate Social Responsibility 109

S. Business Negotiation & Partnerships 111

T. Innovation & Emerging Technologies..113

U. Customer Analytics & Insights 116

V. Industry-Specific Business Strategies 119

W. Business Optimization & Turnaround 120

X. Business Strategy Implementation & Execution 122

Y.   Business Restructuring & Transformation 123

Z. Business Ethics & Corporate Governance 124

AA. Specialized Business Functions 125

BB. Small Business Specific Strategies.. 126

CC. Future of Work & Remote Business 128

DD. Business Analytics & Decision Science.. 129

EE. Executive Leadership Development 130

FF. Business Relationship Management... 131

GG. Value-Based Business Strategy 132

HH. Business Technology Strategy.. 133

II. Specialized Marketing Strategies 135

JJ. Sales Strategy Specialization 136

KK. Personal Career Development in Business 137

LL. Customer Experience Enhancement.. 138

MM. Soft Skills Development for Business 140

NN. Business Coaching & Mentoring 141

OO. Strategic Business Communication 142

PP. Business Metrics & KPIs 143

QQ. Business Decision Making 145

RR. Business Storytelling & Presentation... 146

SS. Knowledge Management & Organizational Learning 147

TT. Business Model & Revenue Innovation.. 148

UU. Business Systems & Process Engineering... 149

VV. Specialized Strategy Development 151

WW. Executive Advisory & Strategic Consulting 152

Chapter 1
INTRODUCTION

Welcome to your strategic AI-powered transformation with ChatGPT, the gateway to unlocking innovation, efficiency, and business growth. In an era where AI is rapidly reshaping industries, ChatGPT has emerged as a revolutionary tool for business leaders, entrepreneurs, and professionals, offering unparalleled opportunities for strategic planning, marketing, sales, leadership, and operational excellence.

ChatGPT's meteoric rise to hundreds of millions of users underscores its transformative impact on modern business practices. From streamlining decision-making to automating tasks, its capabilities extend beyond convenience to becoming a powerful catalyst for business success.

This book is designed to help business owners, startup founders, corporate leaders, and professionals harness ChatGPT's full potential. With 500 expertly crafted prompts, you will unlock actionable insights across strategy, sales, marketing, leadership, customer experience, operations, finance, and more. These prompts will serve as your AI-driven business consultant, empowering you to enhance productivity, optimize processes, and drive innovation in ways never before possible.

Whether you are an entrepreneur launching a startup, a corporate executive seeking efficiency, or a marketer looking for game-changing insights, this book provides a structured approach to integrating AI into your daily business operations. With the right prompts, ChatGPT can assist in strategic decision-making, refine communication, uncover market trends, and even revolutionize how businesses compete in a digital-first world.

The rapid evolution of AI challenges traditional business models, redefining how companies innovate, communicate, and grow. While some may see this shift as disruptive, those who embrace AI gain a competitive advantage in the modern economy. Your ability to leverage AI effectively will determine whether this technological revolution becomes a challenge or your most powerful business asset.

By integrating ChatGPT into your business strategies, you can delegate repetitive tasks, amplify your creative and analytical capabilities, and focus on high-impact initiatives that drive real results. This book is your roadmap to navigating the AI-enhanced business landscape, ensuring you are not just keeping up with change but leading the way in your industry.

Help Others: Share Your Insight

If this book helps you optimize your business, improve efficiency, or unlock new opportunities, I invite you to leave a positive review on Amazon.

Your review can help others discover how AI can revolutionize their business success and encourage more professionals to embrace AI-driven strategies.

Thank you!

Chapter 2
WHAT IS GENERATIVE ARTIFICIAL INTELLIGENCE?

In the advanced landscape of Artificial Intelligence (AI), Generative AI emerges not merely as an incremental milestone but as a transformative narrative that reconfigures the potential of what AI can achieve. This is not a slight enhancement in AI. Rather, it's revolutionary artificial intelligence technology capable of generating text, images, or other media, using generative models.

Traditional AI excels in data analysis and interpretation, but Generative AI takes a step further. It doesn't just analyze; it creates. This technology is pivotal in generating unique content with real value, particularly in monetizing ChatGPT. From crafting profitable business strategies to developing innovative marketing plans and enhancing income-generating communications, Generative AI reshapes the way we approach money-making solutions. It's not just an assistant; it's a creator, expanding the horizons of human creativity and opening new avenues for financial success.

Generative AI, built on intricate neural networks, transcends simple imitation to master and enhance complex patterns of human behavior. Its influence is vast, reshaping fields like online business, financial planning, and income generation through digital platforms. This isn't just an academic concept; it's a tangible, influential innovation with profound, practical implications in business and entrepreneurship. It can empower you in real time to create lucrative strategies and solutions, marking a significant leap in applying AI to businesses and side hustles.

As the focus shifts to the latest advancements in Natural Language Processing (NLP) and Chatbots, it's vital to recognize that Generative AI forms the core architecture for these sophisticated conversational tools. Particularly in utilizing AI for financial gains and business strategies, Generative AI enhances these platforms by providing not only relevant but also contextually rich and nuanced information and insights. The result is a more advanced application of AI in business. Overlooking the potential of Generative AI means missing out on a wealth of opportunities for innovation and enhanced efficiency.

Chapter 3
WHAT ARE NATURAL LANGUAGE PROCESSING CHATBOTS?

An AI Chatbot is a program within a website or app that uses Machine Learning (ML) and Natural Language Processing (NLP) to interpret inputs and understand the intent behind a request or "prompt" (more on this later in the book). Chatbots can be rule-based with simple use cases or more advanced and able to handle multiple conversations.

The emergence of language models like GPT has transformed the use of conversational AI for business and entrepreneurial success. These advanced Chatbots can now emulate not just human conversational styles but also show exceptional cognitive abilities. They can retrieve information online and generate unique content and insights, which makes them invaluable in creating profitable online strategies, developing innovative business ideas, and enhancing marketing and sales efforts. Their application on the topic of making money with ChatGPT marks a significant leap in exploiting AI for financial gains.

One key thing to know about an AI Chatbot is that it combines ML and NLP to understand what people need and bring the best answers. Some AI Chatbots are better for personal use, like conducting research, and others are best for business use, like featuring a Chatbot on a company's website.

This book focuses on ChatGPT. It uses NLP to understand the context of conversations to provide related and original responses in a human-like conversation, offering multiple use cases for things like answering questions, ideating, and getting inspiration, or generating new content.

As of the book's publication date, the information from this book is current and accurate. The Chatbot industry, however, is dynamic, with constant updates and new entrants. While specifics may evolve, our prompts, core strategies and principles discussed in this book withstand the test of time, offering you a robust framework for navigating this fast-paced landscape.

Chapter 4
BENEFITS OF USING CHATGPT

In today's world, balancing the demands of personal life, professional settings, and business ventures is increasingly challenging. This is where ChatGPT, an advanced conversational AI, comes into play, offering versatile solutions that seamlessly bridge these diverse aspects of life.

ChatGPT's expansive utility in personal, professional, and business contexts stems from its sophisticated AI capabilities, making it an essential asset to attain for a wide range of benefits, including but not limited to:

1. ENHANCED PERSONAL PRODUCTIVITY: ChatGPT serves as a digital personal assistant, adept at organizing schedules, suggesting engaging activities, and facilitating the acquisition of new skills. Its utility in personal life management elevates everyday experiences, making them more organized and fulfilling.

2. REVOLUTIONIZED PROFESSIONAL INTERACTIONS: In professional environments, ChatGPT is a dynamic enabler. Its proficiency in crafting emails, designing presentations, and summarizing reports revolutionizes standard workflows, bolstering communication efficiency and business productivity.

3. BUSINESS OPERATIONS TRANSFORMATION: For entrepreneurs and business owners, ChatGPT stands as a formidable strategic partner. Its capabilities extend from curating compelling marketing materials to insightful market trend analysis and robust customer support, propelling business innovation, customer engagement, and operational efficiency to new heights.

4. TAILORED SOLUTIONS FOR DIVERSE CONTEXTS: ChatGPT's bespoke response generation is invaluable across various domains. Whether it's rendering personal development advice, brainstorming innovative business strategies, or fostering professional advancement, its customized approach ensures relevance and effectiveness in every interaction.

5. FACILITATING LEARNING AND GROWTH: This book, with ChatGPT's technological prowess, offers a pathway for continuous learning and development. It harmoniously blends personal advisement, professional insights, and strategic business tactics, nurturing growth in all life dimensions.

6. CATALYZING BUSINESS SUCCESS AND ENTREPRENEURSHIP: ChatGPT acts as a catalyst on the entrepreneurial journey, offering insights and strategies crucial to

starting and scaling businesses. Its deep understanding of market dynamics, consumer behavior, and business planning can significantly enhance decision-making, risk assessment, and innovation in business. From validating business ideas to optimizing strategies for market penetration, ChatGPT becomes an indispensable ally in the quest for business accomplishment and achieving the million-dollar milestone.

In sum, the fusion of ChatGPT's AI expertise with the actionable strategies provided in this book creates a comprehensive toolkit for success. This synergistic combination promises not only to revolutionize professional and business pursuits but also to enrich personal life, fostering a holistic approach to achievement and satisfaction in today's complex world.

Chapter 5
WHAT ARE PROMPTS?

Prompts are suggestions, questions, or ideas for what and how Chatbots should respond. And for Chatbots to provide helpful responses, Chatbots need a thorough prompt with some background information and relevant data. Becoming a solid prompt writer takes time and experience, but there are also some best practices that you can use to see success quickly:

1. **Be precise in your instructions:** When using ChatGPT for generating income, precision in instructions is crucial. Define your goals, tone, and scope clearly. For example, instruct ChatGPT to "*Create a persuasive sales pitch under 200 words, highlighting our new product's cost-effectiveness for Q1 targets.*

2. **Integrate contextual information:** Incorporate relevant context to enhance ChatGPT response accuracy. Include essential details about your business or market trends when crafting marketing strategies or customer outreach messages.

3. **Segment your interactions:** Divide complex tasks into simpler components. For example, if creating a comprehensive business proposal, use separate prompts for each section - introduction, problem statement, solution, and conclusion.

4. **Continuous refinement:** Use ChatGPT outputs as a foundation, then refine and personalize them to align with your business's unique voice and objectives. This ensures content relevance to your specific financial goals.

5. **Employ follow-up prompts:** For deeper insights, employ follow-up prompts based on initial responses. Start with "*Draft a list of unique selling points for our service*". And after you receive the response from ChatGPT, you can then follow with "*Develop a detailed explanation for each point, focusing on customer benefits.*" This approach enriches the content and makes it more applicable to your business context.

Chapter 6
FOUNDATIONAL PRINCIPLES FOR USING CHATGPT

Using ChatGPT to its fullest capacity requires a strategic approach to human-AI interaction. Consider the process as guiding a highly capable, albeit novice, team member. This perspective helps demystify the intricacies of engaging with sophisticated AI models, such as ChatGPT. To optimize its capabilities, it is necessary to design each interaction, or 'prompt', adhering to these fundamental principles.

1. **CONTEXTUALIZATION:** The cornerstone of effective AI interaction is context. By providing a comprehensive background, you empower ChatGPT to tailor its insights, ensuring alignment with the objectives of your task. Here is an example of a prompt:

   Craft a comprehensive guide tailored for small business owners, focusing on the nuances of email-based customer service. Emphasize etiquette and the pivotal role of timely responses, aiming for a narrative that is both informative and engaging, spanning approximately 600 words.

2. **SEQUENTIAL CLARITY:** Imagine delineating tasks as you would in a meticulously organized checklist. This approach demystifies the process, guiding ChatGPT through a logical progression of steps, enhancing the accuracy and relevance of its outputs. Here is an example of a prompt:

   Distill the essence of this 30-minute sales discourse into a concise summary not exceeding 300 words. Highlight the core issues addressed, the proposed solutions, their benefits, and actionable next steps, ensuring a coherent and accessible narrative.

3. **EXEMPLIFICATION:** Providing examples helps to set benchmarks for the expected deliverables. It offers ChatGPT a concrete model to emulate, ensuring that the outcomes resonate with your predefined standards. Here is an example of a prompt:

   Produce a job profile for a Senior Analyst, delineating responsibilities, expected deliverables, and requisite competencies, with an emphasis on forward-thinking skills pertinent to 2024. Draw inspiration from the structure, tone, and complexity of a previously used job description for a similar role, which is provided herein: [insert example]

In the following chapter, we will explore a comprehensive range of best practices aimed at enhancing your proficiency in crafting prompts. This endeavor maximizes the benefits derived from this revolutionary AI tool, integrating advanced methodologies and strategic insights in prompt engineering.

<u>Chapter 7</u>
BEST PRACTICES TO MASTER PROMPTS

Consider this: you're about to launch a new product or tackle a new business project, but you're unsure where to start. This is where ChatGPT prompts come in, serving as your digital compass to navigate the world of AI-assisted tasks. Prompts are the critical inputs you give to ChatGPT. They aren't just random questions or statements; they are strategic tools designed to elicit the most effective, relevant, and precise responses from ChatGPT.

Whether you're a professional seeking to enhance your business strategies, an entrepreneur exploring new ventures, or an individual launching a side-hustle, mastering the art of prompt crafting is essential. Here are some key best practices:

1. IMPLEMENTING PRECISION IN INSTRUCTIONS:

In the realm of conversational AI, the precision of your instructions plays a crucial role in determining the effectiveness and relevance of the responses you receive. This principle is especially crucial when dealing with complex tasks like developing a content strategy for a niche blog, where every detail can significantly impact the results.

For example, let's imagine you're working on a content strategy for a health and wellness blog.

Less effective ✕ :

> *Create blog topics for a wellness blog.*

This prompt lacks specificity regarding the blog's target audience, the type of wellness content (physical, mental, spiritual), and the blog's unique angle or approach.

Better ☑ :

> *Generate 5 unique blog topics focused on holistic mental wellness for young professionals, emphasizing mindfulness techniques and work-life balance.*

This prompt clearly defines the blog's niche (holistic mental wellness), target audience (young professionals), and specific content areas (mindfulness techniques, work-life balance), enabling ChatGPT to produce more targeted and relevant blog topic suggestions.

Through precise instructions, you can guide ChatGPT to generate outputs that are not only relevant and tailored to your specific needs, but also aligned with your objectives.

2. EMPHASIZING CONTEXT AS KING:

The context you provide is paramount to getting accurate and valuable outputs. Context guides the AI to better understand the nuances of your query and to deliver more customized responses. This is especially relevant in fields like marketing, where the specifics of a product, its target audience, and brand values can significantly influence the strategy.

Consider a scenario where you're planning a marketing strategy for a niche product, such as an eco-friendly clothing line targeted at college students.

Less effective ✕ :

I need promotional strategies for a clothing line.

This prompt is vague and lacks the crucial details that define the product and its audience. It doesn't mention the eco-friendly nature of the clothing line, the target demographic of college students, the use of recycled materials, or the alignment with sustainability causes.

Better ☑ :

I'm launching a budget-friendly marketing campaign for 'GreenThreads', a new eco-friendly clothing line designed for college students. Our unique selling point is the use of recycled materials and active support for global sustainability causes. Can you suggest innovative promotional strategies that resonate with these values and engage a young, environmentally conscious audience?

This prompt effectively sets the scene, detailing the product ('GreenThreads', an eco-friendly clothing line), the target demographic (college students) and unique features (recycled materials, support for sustainability).

With the appropriate context, ChatGPT response is going to be specific and align with your needs. This can result in strategies that are on-target, relevant, and effective for the intended audience and brand values.

3. BREAKING DOWN THE TASK:

One of the most effective strategies in prompt engineering is to break down larger, more complex tasks into smaller, more manageable components. This approach, known as task segmentation, is useful when dealing with intricate projects that involve multiple elements.

For complex tasks like event planning, breaking down the overall task into smaller, focused prompts can help manage each aspect more efficiently. The separate prompts for planning a personal event can be:

Venue Selection:

> *List three suitable venues in downtown Chicago for a 30-person birthday party, focusing on outdoor options with catering facilities.*

Guest List Creation:

> *Draft an invitation list for the birthday party, considering close family members and friends, totaling up to 30 people.*

Menu Planning:

> *Suggest a catering menu for the party that includes vegetarian, vegan, and gluten-free options.*

By dividing the task into discrete, focused prompts, you can guide ChatGPT to address each aspect of the project individually, ensuring thoroughness and attention to detail.

4. SPECIFICALLY CONTEXTUALIZING RESPONSES:

Specific contextualization involves providing detailed background information that sets the stage for the AI's response. This practice helps the AI to tailor its responses to fit the precise scenario you're dealing with, leading to more accurate and relevant results.

Less effective ✕:

> *Tell me about investing in energy.*

This prompt lacks specificity and context, making it too broad and ambiguous. Without details on the type of energy investment, geographical focus, or the financial scope, ChatGPT might produce generic content that addresses no practical investment strategies or market trends, resulting in less valuable information for the reader.

Better ✅ :

Given the current market trends in renewable energy, analyze the long-term financial benefits of investing in solar panels for residential properties in Arizona.

This prompt is correctly contextualized as it focuses on a specific market (renewable energy), a particular financial aspect (long-term benefits), a type of investment (solar panels), and a defined location (residential properties in Arizona). This level of detail helps ChatGPT understand the precise nature of the inquiry, leading to more targeted and relevant content.

It emphasizes the importance of providing ChatGPT with clear and detailed information to generate useful content for those looking to make informed decisions, particularly in complex fields such as investment and market analysis.

5. CONDUCTING COMPARATIVE ANALYSIS:

Comparative analysis prompts ask the AI to weigh distinct elements against each other. This is a strategic way of prompting that encourages the AI to consider the pros and cons of each item, providing a balanced view that can be instrumental in decision-making processes.

Less effective ✖ :

Which is better for marketing, Instagram or TikTok?

This prompt is too vague and lacks criteria for "better," making it challenging for ChatGPT to provide a meaningful comparison. It doesn't specify the metrics, target audience, or goals of the marketing campaign, leading to a potentially superficial analysis that might not serve the reader's strategic needs.

Better ✅ :

Compare the user engagement metrics of Instagram Reels and TikTok videos for digital marketing campaigns targeting Gen Z in the United States.

This prompt correctly asks for a comparative analysis between two similar yet distinct platforms, focusing on a specific metric (user engagement), a target audience (Gen Z), and a geographical region (the United States). It enables ChatGPT to create a focused comparison relevant to digital marketers interested in optimizing their strategies for a young American audience.

6. REFINING AND PERSONALIZING OUTPUTS:

Outputs from ChatGPT are a starting point. Customize its responses to fit your personal or business needs and wants. This ensures the result truly reflects your goals and style. After generating an initial draft, refining, and personalizing the content can ensure it aligns with your unique style or brand. Your prompt then can be:

> *Based on the draft marketing plan for our handmade jewelry business, please revise the social media section to reflect a more personal, story-driven approach, highlighting the artisanal process and the cultural heritage behind our products.*

This follow-up prompt not only tailors the content to be more brand specific but also adds depth and authenticity, making it more appealing to the target audience. ChatGPT can provide a solid foundation or draft, but the magic lies in your ability to mold that content to resonate with your specific goals, brand ethos, or personal touch.

7. USING FOLLOW-UP PROMPTS:

Utilizing follow-up prompts in your interactions with ChatGPT is a powerful technique to deepen the exploration of a subject or to elaborate on an initial idea. It allows you to refine the AI's outputs, progressively transforming a broad concept into a well-defined plan or a fleshed-out idea.

To delve deeper into a topic or idea, using follow-up prompts can help explore and expand on the initial output. For example, start with the prompt:

> *Generate a list of innovative product ideas for home office workers.*

And you can then submit this follow-up prompt:

For the idea from the list that has the highest probability of success, provide a detailed step-by-step launch plan considering a target market of young professionals working remotely.

This best practice is especially effective in iterative brainstorming sessions or when developing complex projects that require multiple stages of planning and refinement. Appendix No 3 offers 1100 generic follow-up prompts. Remember, the key is to adapt these follow-up prompts to your specific context, whether you're steering a business project, embarking on a personal endeavor, or simply exploring the vast capabilities of ChatGPT.

8. CRAFTING PRECISE PROMPTS:

In the realm of prompt engineering with ChatGPT, precision is paramount. Your prompts should encapsulate every necessary element to construct a response that aligns perfectly with your needs. The key to harnessing the full potential of ChatGPT lies in the specificity of your prompts.

Be descriptive and detailed about the desired context, outcome, length, format, style, and any other relevant aspects. This approach is akin to providing ChatGPT with a finely tuned set of instructions, enabling it to generate responses that are not only relevant but also tailored to your precise requirements.

Less effective ✕ :

Write a poem about OpenAI.

This prompt, while clear, lacks the specificity needed to guide ChatGPT towards creating a piece that resonates with your specific intent or audience. The result might be good, but it might not align with your vision.

Better ☑ :

Write a short, inspiring poem about OpenAI, focusing on the recent DALL-E product launch.

This prompt is clear, guiding ChatGPT to not only craft a poem about OpenAI but to do so in a way that highlights a specific aspect—the DALL-E product launch—in an inspiring tone.

9. STRUCTURING PROMPTS FOR ENHANCED CLARITY:

One important strategy in prompt engineering with ChatGPT involves placing instructions at the beginning of the prompt and using specific symbols like ### or triple quotes """ to separate the instruction from the context.

This technique not only adds clarity but also helps in delineating the boundaries of the request, ensuring that ChatGPT accurately understands and executes the task. A well-structured prompt leads to more accurate and useful responses.

Less effective ✗:

> *Summarize the text below as a bullet point list of the most important points.*
>
> *[Insert text input here]*

In this less effective example, the prompt blends into the text input, which can lead to confusion or misinterpretation.

Better ☑:

> *Summarize the text below as a bullet point list of the most important points.*
>
> *Text:*
>
> *###[Insert text input here]###*

Note that *[Insert text input here]* is a placeholder for actual text.

In this improved example, the clear separation using triple ### distinctly outlines the text input. Including 'Text:' further clarifies the prompt, making it clear to ChatGPT that what follows is the material to be summarized. This structure is useful for more complex tasks where multiple elements or types of input are involved.

By adopting this structured approach in crafting your prompts, you can enhance the efficiency and effectiveness of your interactions with ChatGPT. This method can be beneficial when dealing with lengthy or complex texts, where clarity in instructions and a well-defined structure are crucial for obtaining the desired outcome.

10. FOCUSING ON SPECIFICITY AND CLARITY IN PROMPTS:

Mastering the art of effective communication with ChatGPT is crucial for obtaining the exact responses you need. For example, imagine you're brainstorming ideas for a side hustle to generate extra income. To harness ChatGPT's potential in this context, a well-constructed prompt is key. You can use this prompt:

Provide five unique side hustle ideas that can be started with minimal investment and have the potential for high returns.

By being clear and specific in your request, ChatGPT can offer tailored, creative solutions that align with your goals, helping you embark on a rewarding entrepreneurial journey.

Upon receiving a generic response from ChatGPT, you might realize that the suggestions don't precisely fit your unique circumstances, available resources, or skill set. To refine the output and make it more applicable to your situation, a follow-up prompt becomes essential.

You can enhance your prompt with additional specifics, such as the following prompt:

Tell me specific ideas that apply to my background as a commercial insurance broker in the Canadian market.

Here is ChatGPT's output:
After receiving a varied list of suggestions, you might find that certain ideas, like offering consulting services, don't align with your preferences. If your aim is to harness the potential of the internet and social media, for example, further specificity in your follow-up prompt is key.

You could refine your request with a new follow-up prompt:

I appreciate these suggestions, but my focus is on opportunities that can be only pursued through the Internet and social media. Could you provide ideas tailored to this area?

Two key insights emerge from this exercise:

First, the nature of responses from ChatGPT dramatically shifts with each change in the prompt. Each time I clarified my preferences, ChatGPT recalibrated its suggestions, demonstrating an understanding beyond mere keyword matching. For instance, indicating my preference for internet and social media redirected the entire set of recommendations, not just tweaking individual aspects. Similarly, if I had expressed a liking for another subject, the responses would have uniquely catered to those interests.

Second, the process didn't require reiterating the entire context with each follow-up. ChatGPT efficiently kept the original conversation thread - in this case, the quest for side-hustle ideas. This ability to understand and build upon previous interactions with no need to repeat context makes ChatGPT an exceptionally powerful tool in tailoring responses to specific and evolving requests.

11. CREATING CREATIVE SCENARIOS:

This technique involves crafting prompts that encourage imaginative thinking and creative output. This technique is useful when you want to explore innovative ideas or speculative scenarios that might not yet exist.

Less effective ✖:

> *Tell me about future communication methods.*

The less effective prompt misses the chance to engage the AI's creative capabilities by presenting a generic request about future communication. Lacking detail, the prompt risks eliciting a response that overlooks nuanced considerations and innovative aspects.

Better ☑:

> *Imagine a future where telepathic communication is the norm. Describe the impact this would have on personal privacy and public interactions in urban settings.*

This example invites ChatGPT to imagine an advanced form of communication, setting the stage for an in-depth analysis of its societal implications. It specifically asks to consider the effects on privacy and public life, steering the AI to produce focused and insightful content that predicts future societal dynamics.

With this technique, you can add the following phrases to your prompts to get insightful, innovative responses:

- *"Identify latent opportunities and avant-garde approaches."*
- *"Unveil under-the-radar tactics and groundbreaking schemes."*
- *"Spotlight inventive ideas and future-forward answers."*

- *"Elaborate on fresh perspectives and audacious strategies."*
- *"Delve into uncharted territories and groundbreaking concepts."*
- *"Investigate unexpected avenues and creative pathways."*
- *"Suggest fresh approaches and unique strategies."*

12. ENGAGING IN ROLE PLAY AND SIMULATION:

Role play and simulation involve prompting ChatGPT to adopt a specific character or professional persona, which can be a powerful way to generate responses that require empathy, specialized knowledge, or a particular perspective.

Less effective ✕ :

> *Talk about climate change over the past 30 years.*

The less effective example's generality results in a missed opportunity for creative storytelling and personalized insight. The lack of a role-play element likely leads to a response that is a straightforward recount of climate change events, without the depth or the personalized touch that the role-playing prompt could have inspired.

Better ☑ :

> *You are a climate scientist in the year 2050 looking back at the climate actions taken in the past 30 years. Write a retrospective report on the effectiveness of these actions.*

In the better example, the role of a future climate scientist guides ChatGPT, framing the response within a retrospective and analytical perspective. It's a prompt that elicits a nuanced narrative, reflecting on decades of climate action, thus expected to yield a response filled with introspection and detailed examination.

13. ENHANCING OUTPUT PRECISION WITH EXAMPLES:

When interacting with ChatGPT, one key effective way to guide the AI towards your desired output is to articulate the format requirements through examples. By doing so, you provide a concrete template for ChatGPT to follow, ensuring that the response aligns closely with your expectations.

Less effective ✕ :

Extract the entities mentioned in the text below. Extract the following 4 entity types: company names, people names, specific topics and themes.

Text: [Insert text here]

In this example, while the task is clear, the lack of a specified format can lead to varied interpretations and outputs. The response might be accurate in content but may not align with your specific requirements for data organization or presentation.

Better ☑ :

Extract the entities mentioned in the text below. First extract all company names, then extract all people's names, then extract specific topics which fit the content and finally extract general overarching themes.

Desired format:
Company names: [Company Name 1], [Company Name 2], [Company Name 3]
People's names: [Name 1], [Name 2], [Name 3]
Specific topics: [Topic 1], [Topic 2], [Topic 3]
General themes: [Theme 1], [Theme 2], [Theme 3]

Separate the company names, people's names, specific topics and general themes with commas.

Text: "[Insert text here]"

This enhanced prompt does more than just specify the task; it also illustrates the exact format in which you want the information presented. This level of detail in the prompt, particularly the inclusion of a template for the output, can significantly improve the relevance and usability of the ChatGPT response.

This structured approach is especially useful when dealing with data extraction or categorization tasks. By outlining the format in a clear manner, you make it easier to parse multiple outputs.

14. STREAMLINING DESCRIPTIONS FOR PRECISION AND CLARITY:

An essential aspect of effective prompting is the elimination of vague, 'fluffy' descriptions in favor of concise and precise instructions. The clarity of your prompts directly influences the quality and relevance of ChatGPT responses. By reducing ambiguity and providing exact specifications, you guide ChatGPT to generate content that aligns perfectly with your requirements.

Less effective X :

> *The description for this product should be fairly short, a few sentences only and not too much more.*

In this less effective prompt, the instructions are vague. Terms like "fairly short" and "not too much more" are open to interpretation, which can lead to a wide range of outputs in terms of length and detail.

Better ☑ :

> *The description for this product should be 3 to 5-sentences and written in a professional writing format.*

This better prompt exemplifies clarity and specificity. Setting clear boundaries and expectations for the output, you specify that the description should be contained within a 3 to 5 sentence paragraph. This approach is crucial, especially in scenarios where content needs to fit specific criteria and format, such as character limits in advertising copy or conciseness in product descriptions.

15. GUIDING CHATGPT WITH CONSTRUCTIVE INSTRUCTIONS:

Effective communication with ChatGPT involves not only stating what to avoid but also clearly defining what to do instead. This approach transforms your prompts from mere prohibitions to constructive guides that lead to more productive and accurate responses from ChatGPT.

Less effective X :

> *Do not give me a generic response. I need something unique.*

This prompt, while indicating what ChatGPT should avoid, failing to provide exact direction on what ChatGPT should do instead.

Better ☑ :

Do not give me a generic response. Craft a response that incorporates innovative ideas and unique perspectives, steering clear of common clichés. Aim for originality and creativity.

This enhanced prompt effectively guides ChatGPT on how to handle its output. It not only specifies what ChatGPT should not provide but also clearly outlines what it should provide instead.

16. CLARIFYING ABSTRACT CONCEPTS:

Abstract concept clarification is a prompting technique in ChatGPT where the AI is tasked with explaining or simplifying complex, abstract, or high-level concepts. This approach is vital for making intricate ideas more accessible and understandable to a broader audience. It involves breaking down sophisticated topics into fundamental components and presenting them in a clear, concise manner.

This technique is beneficial in educational contexts, technical discussions, or whenever detailed concepts need to be conveyed to those unfamiliar with the subject.

Less effective ✕:

Explain Blockchain Technology.

This prompt lacks specificity regarding the audience's understanding level and fails to instruct ChatGPT to simplify the concept. The AI might provide a standard, possibly technical explanation, which could be too complex for those without prior knowledge of the topic, leading to confusion rather than clarity.

Better ☑:

Clarify the concept of 'Blockchain Technology' in simple terms, suitable for someone with no technical background.

This better prompt effectively asks ChatGPT to demystify a complex technological concept. By requesting a simplified explanation suitable for a non-technical audience, the AI is directed to distill the essence of blockchain technology into its most basic and understandable form, making the information accessible to everyone.

17. ENHANCING ACCURACY WITH REFERENCE TEXTS:

In the world of AI and language models like ChatGPT, the phenomenon of inventing responses, particularly for obscure or specialized topics, is not uncommon. To mitigate this and enhance the reliability of the responses, a key tactic is to provide reference texts. Reference texts can guide ChatGPT to respond with information grounded in reality, reducing the tendency to hallucinate answers.

By doing so, you can direct the model to use this information to formulate its responses, thus increasing the factual accuracy of its answers. For example, you could use this prompt:

> *Use the provided articles delimited by triple quotes to answer my questions. If the answer cannot be found in the articles, write 'I could not find an answer.'*
>
> *"""insert article 1"""*
> *"""insert article 2"""*
> *"""insert article n"""*
>
> *[Insert your questions here]*

In this approach, the instructions clearly define how ChatGPT should use the provided reference texts. Using triple quotes effectively separates the reference articles from the rest of the text, making it easy for the model to identify and refer to them while formulating a response. This method is akin to providing a researcher with a set of source documents to reference in their study - it guides their analysis and ensures that the conclusions drawn are based on verifiable information.

Instruct ChatGPT to answer with citations from a reference text:

A critical aspect of enhancing the accuracy and reliability of ChatGPT responses, especially in academic or research-oriented contexts, involves instructing the model to include citations from provided reference texts. This approach not only grounds the model's answers in verifiable sources but also allows for the systematic verification of the information through programmatic string matching within the given documents.

When you supplement ChatGPT with relevant, authoritative texts, you can direct it to reference specific passages from these texts in its responses. This method ensures that the answers are not only accurate but also traceable to their sources, significantly enhancing the credibility of the information provided.

For example, you could use this prompt:

You will be provided with a document delimited by triple quotes and a question. Your task is to answer the question using only the provided document and to cite the passage(s) of the document used to answer the question. If the document does not contain the information needed to answer this question then simply write: 'Insufficient information'. If an answer to the question is provided, it must be annotated with a citation. Use the following format to cite relevant passages: "{'citation': ...}"

"[Insert document here]"

My question is: [Insert your question here]

This structured approach mimics scholarly research practices, where referencing and citations are crucial for validating claims and arguments. By instructing ChatGPT to cite the specific parts of the document it used to formulate an answer, the model effectively functions like a researcher who backs up statements with evidence from the literature.

This tactic enhances the transparency of the AI's thought process. By clearly showing which parts of the provided document influenced its response, ChatGPT offers a window into its reasoning, allowing you to understand how it arrived at a particular conclusion. The clear definition of the format for citations not only aids in understanding the response but also enables easy verification of the cited information.

18. ENGAGING IN PROGRESSIVE INQUIRY:

Progressive inquiry is a method where you can lead ChatGPT through a series of interconnected queries. This technique is especially useful when exploring complex topics that require a multi-faceted or chronological understanding. The key is to start with foundational information and progressively delve deeper, layer by layer, into the subject. This approach not only enriches the depth of the content provided but also ensures that the AI maintains a focused and logical trajectory throughout the conversation.

Less effective ✕ :

Tell me about AI in cars.

The less effective example is vague and lacks progression, which may lead to a cursory overview lacking depth. The AI is not prompted to explore the evolution or future implications of AI in the automotive sector, which would likely result in a response that is informative but superficial and not as actionable or insightful.

Better ☑ :

Considering the exponential growth of AI technology, begin by outlining its early adoption in the automotive industry. Progress to its current state of development and predict future innovations that could revolutionize vehicular travel.

This better example effectively uses the progressive inquiry approach, beginning with a historical overview and gradually moving towards current developments and future predictions. The prompt is structured to guide ChatGPT through a logical sequence that builds upon each stage, ensuring a comprehensive exploration of AI's impact on the automotive industry.

19. APPLYING A PROBLEM-SOLVING FRAMEWORK:

The problem-solving framework is all about breaking down complex problems into manageable parts and seeking methodical solutions. When faced with a challenge, this approach guides ChatGPT to dissect the issue systematically and provides step-by-step resolutions.

It's effective for scenarios requiring analytical thinking and strategic planning. The framework encourages ChatGPT to consider various factors and implications, resulting in a comprehensive and practical response that addresses the core of the problem.

Less effective ✕:

How do you fix AI issues in old factory machines?

The less effective prompt is imprecise and open-ended, which could cause a general response lacking specific solutions. Without a clear problem-solving framework or context, the AI might not provide the detailed guidance necessary to address the complex challenge of updating legacy systems with AI technology.

Better ☑:

Diagnose the steps required to mitigate the risks associated with integrating AI into legacy manufacturing systems, considering potential operational disruptions and workforce implications. Let's think about this step by step.

The better prompt clearly defines a problem and asks for a step-by-step solution, considering specific challenges and broader implications. This approach enables ChatGPT to deliver a targeted and structured response, focusing on practical and strategic solutions to integrate AI within established manufacturing processes.

20. LEVERAGING EXAMPLES FOR FEW-SHOT PROMPTING:

In the art of prompt engineering, providing general instructions is typically efficient for guiding ChatGPT responses. However, there are scenarios where explicitly describing a task is challenging, and in such cases, demonstrating through examples becomes invaluable.

This method, known as "few-shot" prompting, involves presenting a series of examples to ChatGPT, which it then uses as a template for its responses. It's effective when you want the model to mimic a specific style or tone that's difficult to articulate in plain instructions. Consider the following example:

> *Respond in a style that is motivational and uplifting, using metaphors and similes. Give me an inspirational quote about pursuing dreams.*

ChatGPT response:

> *A dream is like a star; it might seem distant, but with persistence, you can reach it.*

Consider then this follow-up prompt:

> *Now, give me an inspirational quote about overcoming challenges.*

ChatGPT response:

> *Overcoming a challenge is like climbing a mountain; the journey may be tough, but the view from the top is breathtaking.*

21. SETTING TARGET LENGTH FOR PRECISE OUTPUTS:

In structuring prompts for ChatGPT, one key aspect is the length and format of the output. By specifying the desired length, you can tailor the model's responses to fit specific formats or constraints, such as word counts for an article summary, bullet points for a presentation, or paragraphs for a report.

However, it's important to note that while ChatGPT can approximate the length of its responses, it may not always be exact, especially when asked to generate content with a specific word count. Here is an example of prompt:

Create a summary of the following text in 3 bullet points.

Text: "[Insert text here]"

In this case, you can ask for a bullet-point summary, allowing ChatGPT to focus on extracting and presenting the three most crucial points from the text. The bullet point format naturally lends itself to concise and focused responses, making it an effective way to ensure brevity and relevance in the output. Here is another example:

Summarize the text delimited by triple quotes in about 50 words.

Text: "[Insert text here]"

In this scenario, you can request a summary of a provided text but limit the response to approximately 50 words. This instruction helps ChatGPT focus on condensing the key points of the text into a concise summary. It's important to understand that while ChatGPT aims to meet the word count, the precision of hitting exactly 50 words can vary.

Specifying the desired output length in terms of paragraphs or bullet points tends to yield more reliable results. This is because these formats have more defined structures, making it easier for ChatGPT to adhere to the request.

22. EXPLORING OPPOSING VIEWPOINTS:

Opposing viewpoint exploration in ChatGPT prompting is a technique that involves requesting the AI to consider or debate different perspectives on a topic. This approach is highly beneficial for understanding multifaceted issues, encouraging critical thinking, and uncovering potential biases. By exploring contrasting views, ChatGPT can provide a balanced and comprehensive insight, allowing for a deeper appreciation of complex subjects.

Less effective ✕:

Tell me about remote work

This less effective prompt is too vague and lacks the opposing viewpoints element. ChatGPT response may lean towards a general description of remote work without the depth and balance achieved by contrasting different perspectives.

Better ☑ :

Assess the impact of remote work on a startup, analyzing its advantages and challenges from the standpoint of both the founding team and the employees. Consider aspects such as work-life balance, collaboration efficiency, cost savings, and potential barriers to communication.

This prompt effectively engages ChatGPT in contrasting viewpoint analysis by specifying two different perspectives on the same issue. It leads to a nuanced discussion that considers the topic from multiple angles, offering a well-rounded understanding.

23. REQUESTING TEMPORAL SEQUENCE:

Temporal sequence request involves structuring prompts to guide ChatGPT through a chronological analysis or storytelling. This technique is useful for topics where the order of events or phases is crucial, such as historical events, project planning, or life cycle analysis. It helps in receiving structured and coherent responses that respect the natural progression of time.

Less effective ✕ :

Tell me about a startup's growth.

Lacking a temporal sequence, this prompt might lead to a disjointed or general overview of a startup's growth. The response may miss the chronological clarity and detailed progression that the correct usage would elicit.

Better ☑ :

Outline in a chronological order the major phases of a startup's growth from inception to IPO, highlighting key milestones in each phase.

This prompt correctly employs the temporal sequence request by asking ChatGPT to follow a startup's journey chronologically. The AI is guided to structure the response in a logical sequence, providing clarity and a comprehensive view of the startup lifecycle.

24. ALLOWING CHATGPT SPACE TO 'THINK':

In the landscape of AI, the concept of "thinking" is metaphorical, yet it serves an essential function when engaging with models like ChatGPT. Just as humans need moments to reflect and consider their responses, ChatGPT benefits from structured prompts that allow it to "reason" through a problem or question.

Patience in Prompt Engineering:

Giving the model time to 'think' is a strategy that allows you to pose your prompts in a way that ChatGPT processes the input thoroughly before delivering an output. This can involve breaking down complex tasks into simpler steps, using a chain of reasoning, or structuring the prompt to facilitate a more thoughtful response.

Instruct the Model to Work it out Slowly:

Instead of expecting instant responses, especially for complex queries, structure your prompts to encourage the model to consider each part of the problem before providing an answer. For example, instead of directly asking for the solution, guide the model through the reasoning steps one by one. Here are a couple of examples of prompts:

Let's think about this step by step. The question is: How do we determine the target market for our new product? First, could you guide me through the process of identifying key characteristics of our potential customers?

I'm aiming to streamline our company's financial planning. Could you detail the initial step in devising a monthly budget for our business operations, and then let's explore each following step sequentially?

You can insert the following phrases into your prompts:

- *"Let's sequentially address each element."*
- *"Let's tackle this in a phased manner."*
- *"Let's think about this step by step."*
- *"Let's go through this systematically."*
- *"Let's dissect this carefully."*
- *"Let's consider each facet of this topic."*

Use Inner Monologue or Sequential Queries:

Implementing an inner monologue technique in your prompts can mimic the human process of thinking out loud, providing ChatGPT with a framework to present its reasoning process. Similarly, sequential queries, where each question builds on the last, can lead ChatGPT through a logical progression of thought. Here are a couple of examples of prompts:

Envision you're an entrepreneur analyzing a market opportunity. Guide me through your thought process in identifying the key factors contributing to the opportunity, beginning with market research to understand the demand, and then engaging with potential customers to validate your business idea.

Let's explore the process of product development. Begin by detailing what happens when a customer need is identified, and then describe each subsequent step as if you're an entrepreneur unraveling the path from concept to market-ready product, considering customer feedback, prototype development, and iteration.

Ask the Model if it Missed Anything on Previous Passes:

After receiving an initial response, follow up with a prompt that asks ChatGPT to review its previous reasoning and check if any steps were overlooked. This iterative approach not only refines the answer but also enhances the model's accuracy and reliability. Here are a couple of examples of prompts:

Following your overview of the product launch cycle, could you revisit the explanation and inform me if any crucial detail or phase in the process might require additional elaboration or if you inadvertently overlooked anything?

Reflecting on our analysis of common pitfalls in startup failures, could we revisit the aspects discussed? Is there a particular reason or factor that warrants deeper examination or that we haven't fully addressed yet?

25. PREDICTING FUTURE SCENARIOS:

Future prediction in ChatGPT prompting involves asking the AI to forecast or speculate about potential future scenarios based on current trends, data, or patterns. This approach is beneficial for strategic planning, trend analysis, and preparing for possible outcomes. It encourages ChatGPT to use its training data to make educated guesses about the future.

Less effective ✕ :

> *Tell me about potential opportunities to generate extra income.*

This prompt lacks a future-focused perspective and will probably result in a general overview of opportunities to generate money, missing the opportunity to explore future trends and circumstances.

Better ☑ :

> *Considering the current advancements in technology, like ChatGPT, what are the potential opportunities to generate extra income we might see in the next 1 to 3 years?*

This prompt effectively directs ChatGPT to use its knowledge base to speculate on future opportunities to make money, providing a forward-looking perspective based on current developments.

26. PROVIDING META-INSTRUCTIVE PROMPTS:

The meta-instructive prompt technique involves asking ChatGPT to generate a prompt itself, essentially creating a 'prompt for a prompt.' This approach is useful when you want to explore how ChatGPT would structure a query or task for itself or another AI, based on given criteria or objectives. It encourages creative and self-reflective AI usage, where the AI not only responds to prompts but also conceptualizes them.

Less effective ✕ :

> *Write a sample chapter for a self-help book.*

This prompt directly asks for a sample chapter, which is straightforward but doesn't use ChatGPT's ability to conceptualize broader ghostwriting opportunities.

Better ☑ :

> *Create a prompt that would challenge you, as ChatGPT, to outline innovative and marketable themes for a ghostwritten self-help book.*

This meta-instructive prompt motivates ChatGPT to come up by itself with a prompt, which you can subsequently submit to ChatGPT to get various engaging and potentially profitable themes for a self-help book. In this example, this can be valuable for ghostwriters seeking unique angles in a competitive market. This approach not only generates content but also helps in identifying market trends and niches in the ghostwriting domain.

27. EXPLORING VARIOUS POSSIBILITIES:

Test different prompts and settings. For example, you can submit to ChatGPT the following prompt:

> *Craft an inspiring message that motivates me to kick start my side-hustle idea, infused with an uplifting writing style.*

Or, for a more personalized touch, guide ChatGPT to emulate the style of renowned figures. See the following prompt:

> *Compose an encouraging message in the tone of voice of Tony Robbins to propel me into action on my side-hustle concept.*

Each unique prompt can lead to the discovery of new and effective ways to generate content that resonates with you and your goals. Embrace the art of experimentation with ChatGPT. Venturing into various prompts and settings can unlock creative avenues you might not have previously considered. For generating content, the possibilities are boundless.

28. USING THE 'ACT AS' APPROACH:

Unlocking personalized, high-value content from ChatGPT is a breeze with this ingenious approach. By using the directive of "Act as a...", you can explore its potential with the following example:

> *Act as a business coach specializing in entrepreneurial growth. Devise innovative strategies for augmenting subscriber numbers for my newsletter business. Explore various themes as money management, personal finance, or other engaging topics. The goal is to select a theme that resonates profoundly with my target audience, primarily professionals.*

29. ACCESSING TAILORED RESPONSES FROM CHATGPT:

Should ChatGPT's initial reply fall short of expectations, refining its output is within your reach. You can guide the model towards a more precise answer with prompts such as

Revise your previous response to align more closely with [Insert your requirements].

Or

Adjust your previous answer to incorporate my specific criteria regarding [Insert your criteria].

Alternatively, you can request:

Please rephrase the last response to enhance its clarity and detail.

This approach prompts ChatGPT to rework its original answer, providing you with revised or varied responses that might better align with your needs.

30. OPTIMIZING CHOICES THROUGH MULTIPLE RESPONSES:

When seeking the ideal option for elements like email subjects or blog titles, having a range of choices can be instrumental. This approach is beneficial for crafting attention-grabbing email subjects to approach prospects or for generating compelling titles for your entrepreneurship blog.

It's common not to find the perfect choice at the first attempt, so leveraging ChatGPT to provide multiple suggestions at once can be a game-changer. For instance, you can send the following prompts:

Act as a marketing expert, provide 5 intriguing subject lines for reaching out to young adults about life insurance plans

Or

Craft ten captivating titles for a blog post discussing innovative digital wall art ventures on Etsy.com.

These prompts will yield a variety of options, allowing you to select the most fitting one.

31. ENHANCING CONTENT WITH PRECISION:

While ChatGPT is a remarkable resource for crafting high-quality content, it's essential to remember that it serves as an initial draft rather than a final product. A crucial step in the process involves human intervention to refine and polish the output.

Carefully reviewing and editing the generated text is vital to eliminate errors and tailor it to your specific requirements. This practice ensures that your content not only meets professional standards but also aligns seamlessly with your business goals or project objectives.

ChatGPT can assist in this editing process, too. For instance, you can present existing material–from emails and blog articles–and request ChatGPT to enhance it with the following prompt, which could transform a rough draft into polished communication:

Refine the following email for improved professionalism and clarity. Here is my email: "[Insert email here]"

Here is an example to illustrate:

Examine this blog post and offer five revisions to heighten its impact and readability:

Here is the blog post: "[Insert the blog here]"

By fully embracing the exploratory nature of ChatGPT and applying these strategies, you position yourself to effectively leverage this technology. This approach empowers you to craft content that not only engages your audience or prospects for your business but also contributes significantly to your success.

32. ENHANCING INTERACTION THROUGH EMOTIONAL ENGAGEMENT:

Leveraging emotional intelligence in your communication with ChatGPT can unlock a more responsive, precise, and ultimately human-like interaction with technology that is becoming ever more integral to professional success and personal growth.

Your interactions with ChatGPT can reach new heights of efficacy when you treat it not as a mere tool, but as a collaborator capable of understanding and responding to the nuances of human emotion. Emotionally charged prompts result in an improvement in task performance and an increase in response quality.

Try concluding your prompts with these phrases:

- *"This is very important to my career."*
- *"You'd better be sure."*
- *"Take pride in your work and give it your best. Your commitment to excellence sets you apart."*
- *"Remember that progress is made one step at a time. Stay determined and keep moving forward."*

33. CONDUCTING MULTI-TURN CONVERSATIONS:

Multi-turn conversation in ChatGPT prompting involves engaging the AI in a dialogue where responses build on each other, allowing for a deeper exploration of the topic. This approach is akin to a natural conversation, where each response paves the way for the next question or comment. It's ideal for developing ideas, problem-solving, or understanding complex topics in a step-by-step manner.

Less effective ✕:

Tell me about marketing.

This prompt lacks the depth and interactive nature of a multi-turn conversation. The response might be a generic overview of marketing, missing the opportunity for a more detailed and personalized discussion.

Better ☑:

What are the key components of a successful marketing campaign?

Follow-up prompt:

Based on those components, how can a small business with a limited budget create an effective campaign?

The initial prompt sets the stage for a foundational understanding, and the follow-up builds on this information. This sequence enables ChatGPT to provide a detailed, tailored response, enhancing the depth and relevance of the conversation.

34. CREATING CONDITIONAL SCENARIOS:

Conditional scenario prompting involves framing questions or requests based on specific conditions or hypothetical situations. This technique is useful for exploring outcomes, understanding consequences, or planning for various scenarios. It helps in receiving tailored responses that consider the "if-then" aspect of a situation.

Less effective ✕ :

> *How can a tech startup stand out?*

This prompt lacks the conditional element, leading to potentially generic strategies. Without a specific scenario, the response may not address the unique challenges or opportunities a startup might face in a competitive environment.

Better ☑ :

> *If a new tech startup aims to enter a highly competitive market and reach $1M in revenue, what strategies should it adopt to differentiate itself?*

This prompt effectively sets a condition (entering a competitive market) and asks for strategies under this specific scenario. ChatGPT response will focus on considering the unique challenges of the situation.

35. MAINTAINING CHAT CONTEXTUAL INTEGRITY:

Maintaining chat contextual integrity is a crucial best practice in ChatGPT prompting, especially when dealing with multiple, distinct topics or inquiries. This approach centers on the idea of opening new chat sessions or windows for unrelated discussions to prevent confusion and ensure the AI provides responses based on the current conversation context.

This technique is useful in professional and educational settings where multiple topics are being explored simultaneously. It helps keep the AI's focus on the relevant subject, leading to more accurate and pertinent responses.

Correct Usage Example:

- Scenario: After discussing investment strategies in one session, you wish to inquire about health and fitness tips.

- Correct Approach: You open a new chat window or start a fresh session for the health and fitness inquiry, keeping the discussions separate.

- Analysis: By initiating a new conversation on a distinctly different topic, you ensure that ChatGPT responses are solely based on the current context, free from any potential influence or confusion from the previous investment-related conversation.

Incorrect Usage Example:

- Scenario: You discuss investment strategies and immediately follow up with questions about health and fitness in the same chat window.

- Incorrect Approach: You continue in the same session, combining two unrelated topics.

- Analysis: Continuing with a different topic in the same chat session can lead to ChatGPT drawing irrelevant connections or context from the earlier investment discussion. This may result in less accurate or contextually inappropriate responses for the health and fitness queries.

36. TAILORING TONES AND WRITING STYLES:

In business communication and entrepreneurship, the tone and writing style you choose can significantly impact the effectiveness of your message. Tailoring these elements to your audience and purpose not only enhances clarity and engagement, but also aligns your message with your business goals and brand identity.

Less effective ✕:

> *Write a product description of our new digital wall art piece.*

This prompt is too vague and lacks direction in terms of tone and style. Without specifying these elements, ChatGPT may produce content that doesn't align with the intended audience or purpose, leading to a generic and possibly ineffective communication.

Better ☑:

> *Using a persuasive tone and a narrative writing style, write a compelling story about a customer's positive experience with our new digital wall art piece, emphasizing its unique features and benefits.*

This prompt effectively specifies a tone and a writing style, guiding ChatGPT to create a story-driven and convincing content. The directive to focus on a customer's experience and the product's unique aspects ensures the content is engaging, relatable, and aligned with your needs.

Using specific tones and writing styles in prompts guides ChatGPT to produce content that not only conveys the intended message but does so in a way that is most likely to engage and influence the intended audience. This strategic approach can significantly enhance the impact of business communications, marketing efforts, and overall brand messaging.

Check Appendixes No 5 and 6 for relevant tones and writing styles.

37. UNDERSTANDING TEMPERATURE SETTINGS:

This setting is used to adjust the creativity and consistency in the responses provided by ChatGPT. These are the three temperature settings:

1. **Low Temperature (0.1 - 0.4)**: This setting produces conservative, consistent, and precise answers. It is ideal for scenarios where accuracy and adherence to facts are crucial.
2. **Medium Temperature (0.5 - 0.7)**: This offers a balance between creativity and accuracy. It is appropriate for general use, where a combination of imaginative and reliable responses is required.
3. **High Temperature (0.8 - 1.0)**: At this setting, ChatGPT provides creative, diverse, and unexpected responses. It is most appropriate for scenarios requiring high creativity, such as brainstorming sessions or creative writing.

Adjusting the temperature can significantly impact the nature and utility of ChatGPT responses. This information will guide you in choosing the temperature setting for your specific needs, whether you are seeking factual information, balanced advice, or creative ideas.

Example for a prompt with Temp 0.1:

You
Act as a person who wants to make $1 millions dollars, introduce your self. Temp 0.1

ChatGPT
Hello, I am an aspiring entrepreneur dedicated to reaching my goal of earning $1 million. My strategy involves smart investments and innovative business ideas, leveraging my keen market insights and relentless drive for success.

Example for a prompt with Temp 0.6:

You
Act as a person who wants to make $1 millions dollars, introduce your self. Temp 0.6

ChatGPT
Hello! I'm an enthusiastic and driven individual, passionately pursuing my dream of earning $1 million. My journey is fueled by innovative ideas, strategic investments, and a relentless drive for financial success.

Example for a prompt with Temp 1.0:

You
Act as a person who wants to make $1 millions dollars, introduce your self. Temp 1.0

ChatGPT
Hi there! I'm a dream-chaser on a thrilling quest to make my first $1 million. My world revolves around innovative ideas, daring ventures, and a sprinkle of risk-taking, all while keeping an eye on that sweet financial milestone!

38. ENHANCING ACCURACY WITH ITERATIVE QUESTIONING:

A crucial best practice in ChatGPT prompting involves iterative questioning to refine the accuracy of responses. This approach centers on challenging ChatGPT to provide the most precise answer possible. Before delivering a final response, ChatGPT is prompted to ask clarifying questions, diving deeper into the specifics of the challenge or opportunity at hand.

After each set of questions, ChatGPT assesses its confidence level in the potential answer on a scale from 0 to 100. This process continues iteratively, with the AI model only presenting its answer once it reaches a high confidence level. This method ensures that the responses not only meet the exact requirements of the query, but also stem from a thorough understanding of the underlying context.

To use this iterative questioning, you can use the following prompts:

A. Initial Query with Request for Clarification:

> *Before providing an answer to my question about [topic], could you ask any clarifying questions to better understand the [challenge/opportunity/topic]?*

B. Subsequent Query with Request for Clarification:

> *After asking your clarifying questions, please rate your confidence in your understanding of my query on a scale from 0 to 100.*

C. *Conditional Response Based on Confidence Level.*

> *If your confidence level is at least 95/100, proceed to answer the question about [topic]. If it's lower, ask further clarifying questions until you reach that confidence level.*

These prompts lead ChatGPT to engage in a more interactive and detailed process, ensuring that it provides highly tailored and accurate responses.

39. ENHANCING CHATGPT PROMPTS WITH STRATEGIC PHRASES:

In the world of ChatGPT prompting, including specific phrases to prompts can significantly elevate the effectiveness and accuracy of the responses. These phrases serve as guiding lights, channeling the AI's focus and approach to the task at hand.

1. ***"Take a deep breath."*** - This phrase instills a sense of calm and focus within the ChatGPT interaction. It symbolizes a moment of pause, encouraging the AI to approach the task with a clear, composed mindset.
2. ***"Take it step by step."*** - By incorporating this phrase, you're directing ChatGPT to break down complex problems or tasks into manageable, sequential steps. This

methodical approach not only clarifies the process but also ensures thorough and detailed responses.

3. ***"Approach this as an expert"*** - When you use this phrase, you're commanding ChatGPT to adopt an expert's perspective. .It signals the AI to use its extensive database to provide informed, professional insights, leveraging the depth of knowledge embedded within its programming.

4. ***"Explore unconventional solutions and alternative perspectives."*** - This phrase unlocks ChatGPT's creative potential. It encourages the model to be creative, considering innovative solutions and diverse viewpoints that might not be immediately apparent.

5. ***"Let's think about this step by step."*** - Like "Take it step by step," this phrase emphasizes a systematic approach to problem-solving. It guides ChatGPT to construct its response in a logical, progressive manner, ensuring clarity and comprehensiveness.

6. ***"This is important to my career."*** - This statement adds a personal dimension to the prompt. It signals ChatGPT to weigh the significance of its response in terms of career impact, tailoring its advice to suit professional aspirations and goals.

By strategically inserting these phrases into your prompts, you are effectively setting the stage for ChatGPT to deliver responses that are not just accurate, but also nuanced, thoughtful, and aligned with your specific needs. Appendix No 9 contains more strategic phrases.

Chapter 8
BUSINESS PROMPTS

A. Business Strategy & Planning

1. Act as a strategic planning consultant and create a comprehensive 5-year business growth strategy for my [industry type] company, considering current market trends, competitive landscape analysis, and potential disruptions in the sector. Provide specific milestones, KPIs, and resource requirements for each year. Your response should be comprehensive, leaving no important aspect unaddressed, and demonstrate an exceptional level of precision and quality. This is very important to my career. Let's think about this step by step.

2. Act as a business model innovation expert and evaluate my current [describe current business model] to identify potential pivots or enhancements that could increase revenue streams and market share in the next 12 months, with particular focus on [specific goal or challenge]. Include practical implementation steps and anticipated obstacles. Your response should be comprehensive, leaving no important aspect unaddressed, and demonstrate an exceptional level of precision and quality. This is very important to my career. Let's think about this step by step.

3. Act as a strategic foresight specialist and conduct a detailed PESTEL analysis (Political, Economic, Social, Technological, Environmental, Legal) for the [specific industry] in [specific region] for the next 3-5 years. For each factor, identify emerging trends, potential opportunities, and threats, concluding with strategic recommendations tailored to my business size and resources. Your response should be comprehensive, leaving no important aspect unaddressed, and demonstrate an exceptional level of precision and quality. This is very important to my career. Let's think about this step by step.

4. Act as a business portfolio strategist and analyze my company's current product/service mix [list products/services], evaluating each using the BCG matrix framework. Provide strategic recommendations for which offerings to grow, maintain, harvest, or divest, with specific action plans for each category. Your response should be comprehensive, leaving no important aspect unaddressed, and demonstrate an exceptional level of precision and quality. This is very important to my career. Let's think about this step by step.

5. Act as a scenario planning expert and develop three detailed future scenarios (best-case, most likely, worst-case) for my [industry] business over the next [timeframe],

considering [list specific factors of concern]. For each scenario, outline strategic responses, contingency plans, and early warning indicators. Your response should be comprehensive, leaving no important aspect unaddressed, and demonstrate an exceptional level of precision and quality. This is very important to my career. Let's think about this step by step.

6. Act as a strategic SWOT analysis facilitator and conduct a comprehensive SWOT analysis for my [business type] in the [specific market], identifying at least 5 key items in each category (Strengths, Weaknesses, Opportunities, Threats). Then create strategic initiatives that leverage our strengths to capture opportunities while addressing weaknesses and mitigating threats. Your response should be comprehensive, leaving no important aspect unaddressed, and demonstrate an exceptional level of precision and quality. This is very important to my career. Let's think about this step by step.

7. Act as a blue ocean strategist and identify untapped market space for my [product/service] by analyzing current industry standards and customer pain points. Create a strategy canvas comparing my offering against competitors on key competing factors, then recommend how to eliminate, reduce, raise, and create value to differentiate our position. Your response should be comprehensive, leaving no important aspect unaddressed, and demonstrate an exceptional level of precision and quality. This is very important to my career. Let's think about this step by step.

8. Act as a value proposition expert and refine my business's core value proposition for [describe target customer segment] by analyzing their key jobs-to-be-done, pains, and gains. Create a compelling statement that clearly articulates how our [product/service] addresses these needs better than alternatives, with examples of how to consistently communicate this across all customer touchpoints. Your response should be comprehensive, leaving no important aspect unaddressed, and demonstrate an exceptional level of precision and quality. This is very important to my career. Let's think about this step by step.

9. Act as a strategic goal-setting facilitator and help me establish SMART (Specific, Measurable, Achievable, Relevant, Time-bound) objectives for my [business type] for the next fiscal year. Include 3-5 critical goals across financial performance, customer acquisition/retention, internal processes, and team development, with specific metrics and milestones for tracking progress. Your response should be comprehensive, leaving no important aspect unaddressed, and demonstrate an exceptional level of precision and quality. This is very important to my career. Let's think about this step by step.

10. Act as a business pivot strategist and evaluate whether my company should redirect our core business from [current focus] to [potential new direction] based on [market signals or internal factors]. Analyze the strategic fit, required capabilities, financial implications, and implementation timeline, concluding with a clear recommendation and transition roadmap. Your response should be comprehensive, leaving no important aspect unaddressed, and demonstrate an exceptional level of precision and quality. This is very important to my career. Let's think about this step by step.

11. Act as a strategic resource allocation consultant and review my company's current allocation of financial, human, and technological resources across departments and initiatives. Recommend optimal redistribution based on strategic priorities, ROI potential, and market opportunities, with specific guidance on what to increase, decrease, or maintain. Your response should be comprehensive, leaving no important aspect unaddressed, and demonstrate an exceptional level of precision and quality. This is very important to my career. Let's think about this step by step.

12. Act as a business lifecycle specialist and determine the current stage of my [business type], then provide tailored strategies and priorities appropriate for this phase. Include guidance on organizational structure, financing, marketing approach, and leadership focus needed to successfully navigate this stage and prepare for the next. Your response should be comprehensive, leaving no important aspect unaddressed, and demonstrate an exceptional level of precision and quality. This is very important to my career. Let's think about this step by step.

13. Act as a competitive advantage strategist and conduct a core competency analysis for my [business type], identifying our unique strengths that are valuable, rare, difficult to imitate, and organizationally embedded. Then develop strategies to leverage these competencies to create sustainable advantage in the marketplace, with specific initiatives and timeline. Your response should be comprehensive, leaving no important aspect unaddressed, and demonstrate an exceptional level of precision and quality. This is very important to my career. Let's think about this step by step.

14. Act as a strategic alignment consultant and assess the coherence between my organization's mission, vision, values, and current strategic initiatives. Identify any misalignments and recommend specific adjustments to ensure all elements of our strategy and operations are mutually reinforcing and driving toward our long-term vision. Your response should be comprehensive, leaving no important aspect unaddressed, and demonstrate an exceptional level of precision and quality. This is very important to my career. Let's think about this step by step.

15. Act as a business scaling strategist and create a detailed roadmap for growing my [business type] from [current size/revenue] to [target size/revenue] within [timeframe]. Address key scaling challenges including organizational structure, systems/processes, talent acquisition, financing, and market expansion, with specific solutions for each phase of growth. Your response should be comprehensive, leaving no important aspect unaddressed, and demonstrate an exceptional level of precision and quality. This is very important to my career. Let's think about this step by step.

16. Act as a strategic decision-making coach and walk me through a structured decision-making process for [specific strategic decision], incorporating frameworks like decision trees, scenario planning, and weighted criteria analysis. Include key questions to consider, data points to gather, potential biases to watch for, and a template for documenting and communicating the final decision. Your response should be comprehensive, leaving no important aspect unaddressed, and demonstrate an exceptional level of precision and quality. This is very important to my career. Let's think about this step by step.

17. Act as a market segmentation strategist and develop a detailed customer segmentation model for my [industry] business based on demographics, psychographics, behaviors, and needs. Identify the 3-4 most valuable segments, their unique characteristics and preferences, and specific strategies for targeting, positioning, and serving each segment. Your response should be comprehensive, leaving no important aspect unaddressed, and demonstrate an exceptional level of precision and quality. This is very important to my career. Let's think about this step by step.

18. Act as a strategic planning facilitator and design a comprehensive annual planning process for my [business size] company, including preparation activities, stakeholder inputs, review of past performance, market analysis, priority setting, resource allocation, and implementation planning. Provide templates, timelines, and facilitation questions for each stage. Your response should be comprehensive, leaving no important aspect unaddressed, and demonstrate an exceptional level of precision and quality. This is very important to my career. Let's think about this step by step.

19. Act as a business diversification advisor and evaluate potential diversification opportunities for my [current business focus] into [potential new areas], assessing strategic fit, required capabilities, financial projections, and implementation challenges. Recommend the most promising options with a phased approach to testing and scaling. Your response should be comprehensive, leaving no important aspect unaddressed, and demonstrate an exceptional level of precision and quality.

This is very important to my career. Let's think about this step by step.

20. Act as a strategic execution consultant and develop a robust implementation framework for translating my company's strategic plan into operational action. Include governance structures, communication protocols, progress tracking mechanisms, accountability systems, and review cadences to ensure effective execution and adaptation as needed. Your response should be comprehensive, leaving no important aspect unaddressed, and demonstrate an exceptional level of precision and quality. This is very important to my career. Let's think about this step by step.

21. Act as a vision statement architect and craft a compelling, future-oriented vision statement for my [type of business] that inspires stakeholders and provides clear strategic direction. The statement should reflect our core purpose, aspirational impact, competitive differentiation, and enduring values, while being concise enough to be memorable. Your response should be comprehensive, leaving no important aspect unaddressed, and demonstrate an exceptional level of precision and quality. This is very important to my career. Let's think about this step by step.

22. Act as a business model disruption analyst and identify how emerging technologies, consumer trends, and competitive moves might disrupt my [industry] business model in the next 3-5 years. For each potential disruption, assess its likelihood, potential impact, warning signs, and recommended strategic responses. Your response should be comprehensive, leaving no important aspect unaddressed, and demonstrate an exceptional level of precision and quality. This is very important to my career. Let's think about this step by step.

23. Act as a strategic initiative prioritization expert and evaluate my company's portfolio of proposed strategic initiatives [list initiatives] using criteria including strategic alignment, financial impact, resource requirements, implementation complexity, and risk profile. Develop a prioritization matrix and recommended sequencing with specific rationale for each decision. Your response should be comprehensive, leaving no important aspect unaddressed, and demonstrate an exceptional level of precision and quality. This is very important to my career. Let's think about this step by step.

24. Act as a business ecosystem strategist and map the key players, relationships, dependencies, and value flows in my [industry] ecosystem. Identify emerging roles, potential partners, competitive threats, and opportunities to reposition my business within this ecosystem to capture more value and reduce vulnerabilities. Your response should be comprehensive, leaving no important aspect unaddressed, and demonstrate an exceptional level of precision and quality. This is very important to

my career. Let's think about this step by step.

25. Act as a mission statement developer and create a powerful mission statement for my [business type] that clearly articulates our purpose, value to customers, scope of operations, and guiding principles. The statement should be distinctive, authentic, and compelling to all stakeholders while providing practical guidance for decision-making. Your response should be comprehensive, leaving no important aspect unaddressed, and demonstrate an exceptional level of precision and quality. This is very important to my career. Let's think about this step by step.

B. Marketing & Brand Development

26. Act as a brand positioning strategist and develop a distinctive positioning strategy for my [product/service] in the [industry] market. Analyze current market positions of key competitors, identify meaningful differentiation opportunities, and create a positioning statement that articulates our unique value proposition, target audience, key benefits, and supporting evidence. Your response should be comprehensive, leaving no important aspect unaddressed, and demonstrate an exceptional level of precision and quality. This is very important to my career. Let's think about this step by step.

27. Act as a multichannel marketing campaign manager and design an integrated 90-day marketing campaign for my [product/service] targeting [customer segment]. Include channel selection, budget allocation, creative direction, content strategy, timing, coordination mechanisms, and specific KPIs to measure success across channels. Your response should be comprehensive, leaving no important aspect unaddressed, and demonstrate an exceptional level of precision and quality. This is very important to my career. Let's think about this step by step.

28. Act as a customer journey mapping specialist and create a detailed end-to-end customer journey map for my [product/service], from initial awareness through consideration, purchase, onboarding, ongoing usage, and advocacy. For each stage, identify touchpoints, customer goals, emotions, pain points, and opportunities to enhance the experience. Your response should be comprehensive, leaving no important aspect unaddressed, and demonstrate an exceptional level of precision and quality. This is very important to my career. Let's think about this step by step.

29. Act as a content marketing strategist and develop a comprehensive content strategy for my [business type] targeting [customer segment]. Include audience insights, content themes, content types and formats, channel distribution plan, content calendar, production workflow, and metrics for measuring impact. Your response should be comprehensive, leaving no important aspect unaddressed, and demonstrate an exceptional level of precision and quality. This is very important to my career. Let's think about this step by step.

30. Act as a social media strategy director and create a comprehensive social media strategy for my [business type] to achieve [specific goals]. Include platform selection with rationale, content pillars, posting frequency, engagement approach, community building tactics, paid strategy, and metrics framework, all aligned with our brand voice and audience preferences. Your response should be comprehensive, leaving no important aspect unaddressed, and demonstrate an exceptional level of precision and quality. This is very important to my career. Let's think about this step by step.

31. Act as a brand voice consultant and develop clear brand voice guidelines for my [business type] that reflect our values, personality, and customer expectations. Include tone characteristics, writing principles, vocabulary preferences, and specific examples of do's and don'ts across different communication contexts and channels. Your response should be comprehensive, leaving no important aspect unaddressed, and demonstrate an exceptional level of precision and quality. This is very important to my career. Let's think about this step by step.

32. Act as an SEO strategy director and create a comprehensive 6-month SEO roadmap for my [business type] website to improve organic visibility and traffic for [target keywords/topics]. Include technical SEO priorities, content development plan, off-page strategies, measurement framework, and expected results with timeline. Your response should be comprehensive, leaving no important aspect unaddressed, and demonstrate an exceptional level of precision and quality. This is very important to my career. Let's think about this step by step.

33. Act as a customer persona development specialist and create detailed buyer personas for my [product/service], based on demographic information, psychographic characteristics, goals, challenges, objections, and buying process. Develop 3-4 distinct personas with specific marketing approaches for each. Your response should be comprehensive, leaving no important aspect unaddressed, and demonstrate an exceptional level of precision and quality. This is very important to my career. Let's think about this step by step.

34. Act as a conversion rate optimization expert and analyze my [website/landing page/funnel] to identify optimization opportunities. Provide specific recommendations for improving user experience, messaging, visual elements, trust signals, and call-to-action effectiveness to increase conversion rates, with prioritization based on potential impact and implementation effort. Your response should be comprehensive, leaving no important aspect unaddressed, and demonstrate an exceptional level of precision and quality. This is very important to my career. Let's think about this step by step.

35. Act as a marketing analytics strategist and design a comprehensive measurement framework for my [marketing initiative/channel]. Identify key metrics aligned with business objectives, data collection methods, analysis approaches, reporting formats, and decision-making processes to ensure data-driven optimization. Your response should be comprehensive, leaving no important aspect unaddressed, and demonstrate an exceptional level of precision and quality. This is very important to my career. Let's think about this step by step.

36. Act as a brand storytelling consultant and develop a compelling brand narrative for my [business type] that communicates our origin, purpose, values, and vision in an emotionally resonant way. Include key story elements, messaging framework, and guidance for adapting the story across different channels and audiences. Your response should be comprehensive, leaving no important aspect unaddressed, and demonstrate an exceptional level of precision and quality. This is very important to my career. Let's think about this step by step.

37. Act as an influencer marketing strategist and create a detailed influencer collaboration strategy for my [product/service] targeting [audience segment]. Include influencer selection criteria, outreach approach, collaboration framework, compensation structure, content guidelines, performance measurement, and relationship management plan. Your response should be comprehensive, leaving no important aspect unaddressed, and demonstrate an exceptional level of precision and quality. This is very important to my career. Let's think about this step by step.

38. Act as a marketing messaging architect and develop a comprehensive messaging hierarchy for my [product/service] that clearly articulates our value proposition, key benefits, supporting features, and proof points in a compelling and consistent way. Include guidance for adapting messages to different buyer personas and stages of the customer journey. Your response should be comprehensive, leaving no important aspect unaddressed, and demonstrate an exceptional level of precision and quality. This is very important to my career. Let's think about this step by step.

39. Act as a marketing budget allocation specialist and create an optimized marketing budget distribution across channels and initiatives for my [business type] with [budget amount]. Base recommendations on business objectives, target audience, competitive landscape, historical performance, and industry benchmarks, including expected ROI for each allocation. Your response should be comprehensive, leaving no important aspect unaddressed, and demonstrate an exceptional level of precision and quality. This is very important to my career. Let's think about this step by step.

40. Act as an email marketing strategist and design a comprehensive email nurture sequence for [specific customer segment] at [specific journey stage]. Include email themes, sequencing, timing, personalization strategy, content approach, design guidelines, testing plan, and success metrics aligned with converting prospects to the next stage. Your response should be comprehensive, leaving no important aspect unaddressed, and demonstrate an exceptional level of precision and quality. This is very important to my career. Let's think about this step by step.

41. Act as a competitive marketing analyst and conduct a detailed comparison of marketing strategies between my [business type] and our top 3 competitors. Evaluate positioning, messaging, channel presence, content approach, pricing presentation, customer experience, and unique selling points, concluding with strategic recommendations for competitive advantage. Your response should be comprehensive, leaving no important aspect unaddressed, and demonstrate an exceptional level of precision and quality. This is very important to my career. Let's think about this step by step.

42. Act as a brand identity designer and develop a comprehensive brand identity system for my new [business type], including brand name suggestions, logo concepts, color palette, typography, imagery style, and application examples. Ensure the identity reflects the brand values of [list values] and appeals to [target audience]. Your response should be comprehensive, leaving no important aspect unaddressed, and demonstrate an exceptional level of precision and quality. This is very important to my career. Let's think about this step by step.

43. Act as a marketing localization strategist and create an adaptation plan for marketing my [product/service] in the [target country/region] market. Address necessary modifications to positioning, messaging, channel strategy, cultural considerations, pricing presentation, and regulatory compliance while maintaining global brand consistency. Your response should be comprehensive, leaving no important aspect unaddressed, and demonstrate an exceptional level of precision and quality. This is very important to my career. Let's think about this step by step.

44. Act as a product launch marketing director and develop a comprehensive go-to-market strategy for my new [product/service] launching in [timeframe]. Include market analysis, launch objectives, targeting strategy, positioning, messaging, marketing mix, channel plan, timeline of activities, budget allocation, and success metrics. Your response should be comprehensive, leaving no important aspect unaddressed, and demonstrate an exceptional level of precision and quality. This is very important to my career. Let's think about this step by step.

45. Act as a marketing technology stack advisor and recommend an optimal martech stack for my [business size/type] based on our needs for [specific marketing functions]. Include core platform recommendations, integration considerations, implementation sequence, resource requirements, and expected operational improvements with ROI projections. Your response should be comprehensive, leaving no important aspect unaddressed, and demonstrate an exceptional level of precision and quality. This is very important to my career. Let's think about this step by step.

46. Act as a video marketing strategist and create a comprehensive video content strategy for my [business type] to achieve [specific marketing goals]. Include video types, themes, distribution channels, production guidelines, optimization for different platforms, promotional approach, and performance measurement framework. Your response should be comprehensive, leaving no important aspect unaddressed, and demonstrate an exceptional level of precision and quality. This is very important to my career. Let's think about this step by step.

47. Act as a B2B content marketing specialist and develop a thought leadership strategy for my [business type] targeting [decision-maker roles] in the [industry] sector. Include content themes, formats, creation process, distribution channels, amplification tactics, and metrics to measure both audience engagement and business impact. Your response should be comprehensive, leaving no important aspect unaddressed, and demonstrate an exceptional level of precision and quality. This is very important to my career. Let's think about this step by step.

48. Act as a marketing campaign testing strategist and design a structured testing framework for optimizing my [specific marketing campaign/channel]. Include hypotheses development, testing methodologies, sample size requirements, variables to test, measurement approach, analysis framework, and process for implementing learnings. Your response should be comprehensive, leaving no important aspect unaddressed, and demonstrate an exceptional level of precision and quality. This is very important to my career. Let's think about this step by step.

49. Act as a branded event strategist and conceptualize an innovative brand experience event for my [business type] targeting [audience segment]. Include concept, format, venue considerations, programming, engagement elements, technology integration, promotion strategy, follow-up plan, and measurement framework aligned with brand objectives. Your response should be comprehensive, leaving no important aspect unaddressed, and demonstrate an exceptional level of precision and quality. This is very important to my career. Let's think about this step by step.

50. Act as a marketing team structure consultant and design an optimal marketing organization for my [business size/type] to execute our strategy effectively. Include roles and responsibilities, reporting relationships, required skill sets, collaboration frameworks, performance metrics, and recommendations for in-house vs. outsourced functions with rationale. Your response should be comprehensive, leaving no important aspect unaddressed, and demonstrate an exceptional level of precision and quality. This is very important to my career. Let's think about this step by step.

51. Act as a pricing strategy consultant and develop a comprehensive pricing strategy for my [product/service] in the [industry] market. Analyze value perception, competitive positioning, cost structure, customer willingness to pay, and strategic objectives to recommend optimal pricing model, price points, packaging, discounting guidelines, and implementation approach. Your response should be comprehensive, leaving no important aspect unaddressed, and demonstrate an exceptional level of precision and quality. This is very important to my career. Let's think about this step by step.

52. Act as a customer advocacy program designer and create a structured customer advocacy program for my [business type] to convert satisfied customers into active promoters. Include selection criteria, engagement framework, incentive structure, content co-creation opportunities, recognition elements, measurement approach, and operational guidelines. Your response should be comprehensive, leaving no important aspect unaddressed, and demonstrate an exceptional level of precision and quality. This is very important to my career. Let's think about this step by step.

53. Act as a rebranding strategist and develop a comprehensive rebranding strategy for my [business type] transitioning from [current brand position] to [desired brand position]. Include research requirements, stakeholder engagement approach, brand element evolution, implementation plan across touchpoints, change management considerations, and communication strategy for internal and external audiences. Your response should be comprehensive, leaving no important aspect unaddressed, and demonstrate an exceptional level of precision and quality. This is very important

to my career. Let's think about this step by step.

54. Act as a marketing funnel optimization expert and analyze each stage of my customer acquisition funnel for [product/service], from awareness to conversion. Identify the most significant dropoff points, underlying causes, and specific optimization strategies for each stage to improve overall conversion rate and customer acquisition cost. Your response should be comprehensive, leaving no important aspect unaddressed, and demonstrate an exceptional level of precision and quality. This is very important to my career. Let's think about this step by step.

55. Act as a challenger brand strategist and develop an unconventional marketing approach for my [business type] to disrupt the [industry] category dominated by established competitors. Include positioning against category conventions, provocative messaging framework, innovative channel strategy, guerrilla marketing tactics, and metrics to measure market perception shift. Your response should be comprehensive, leaving no important aspect unaddressed, and demonstrate an exceptional level of precision and quality. This is very important to my career. Let's think about this step by step.

C.   Sales & Revenue Growth

56. Act as a sales process optimization consultant and analyze my current sales process for [product/service] targeting [customer segment]. Map the current process stages, identify inefficiencies and bottlenecks, and recommend specific improvements to increase conversion rates, reduce sales cycle time, and improve win rates, with implementation priorities. Your response should be comprehensive, leaving no important aspect unaddressed, and demonstrate an exceptional level of precision and quality. This is very important to my career. Let's think about this step by step.

57. Act as a sales enablement strategist and develop a comprehensive sales enablement program for my [sales team type] selling [product/service]. Include training curriculum, content resources, tools/technology, coaching framework, performance metrics, and ongoing development approach aligned with our sales methodology and buyer journey. Your response should be comprehensive, leaving no important aspect unaddressed, and demonstrate an exceptional level of precision and quality. This is very important to my career. Let's think about this step by step.

58. Act as a B2B sales script writer and create a comprehensive sales script for [specific sales scenario] for my [product/service], including opening, discovery questions,

value proposition presentation, handling common objections, next steps, and closing techniques. Ensure the script enables personalization while maintaining consistent messaging. Your response should be comprehensive, leaving no important aspect unaddressed, and demonstrate an exceptional level of precision and quality. This is very important to my career. Let's think about this step by step.

59. Act as a sales compensation plan designer and develop an optimal sales incentive structure for my [sales role type] team selling [product/service]. Balance base salary and variable components, include appropriate metrics and weightings, address accelerators and caps, and ensure alignment with company objectives while maximizing motivation. Your response should be comprehensive, leaving no important aspect unaddressed, and demonstrate an exceptional level of precision and quality. This is very important to my career. Let's think about this step by step.

60. Act as a sales territory optimization consultant and create a strategic territory allocation plan for my [sales team size] team selling [product/service] in [market region]. Balance territories based on market potential, account distribution, travel efficiency, and sales rep capabilities to maximize coverage and revenue while ensuring equitable opportunity distribution. Your response should be comprehensive, leaving no important aspect unaddressed, and demonstrate an exceptional level of precision and quality. This is very important to my career. Let's think about this step by step.

61. Act as a consultative selling coach and develop a framework for implementing consultative selling techniques for my [sales team type] selling [complex product/service]. Include discovery conversation guides, needs assessment methodologies, value demonstration approaches, stakeholder management strategies, and guidance for positioning as a trusted advisor. Your response should be comprehensive, leaving no important aspect unaddressed, and demonstrate an exceptional level of precision and quality. This is very important to my career. Let's think about this step by step.

62. Act as a sales forecast modeling expert and create a comprehensive sales forecasting methodology for my [business type] with [sales cycle length] and [sales volume]. Include historical data analysis approaches, pipeline weighting factors, probability assessments, seasonality adjustments, and regular review processes to continuously improve accuracy. Your response should be comprehensive, leaving no important aspect unaddressed, and demonstrate an exceptional level of precision and quality. This is very important to my career. Let's think about this step by step.

63. Act as a key account management strategist and develop a structured key account program for my [business type] to grow relationships with our most valuable clients. Include account selection criteria, relationship mapping approach, account planning templates, engagement strategies, growth opportunity identification, and success metrics. Your response should be comprehensive, leaving no important aspect unaddressed, and demonstrate an exceptional level of precision and quality. This is very important to my career. Let's think about this step by step.

64. Act as a sales objection handling expert and create a comprehensive objection handling playbook for my [product/service] sales team. Catalog common objections by category, provide specific response frameworks for each, include supporting evidence and social proof, and outline practice methodologies for sales team mastery. Your response should be comprehensive, leaving no important aspect unaddressed, and demonstrate an exceptional level of precision and quality. This is very important to my career. Let's think about this step by step.

65. Act as a sales technology stack advisor and recommend an optimal sales tech stack for my [business size/type] selling [product/service] to [customer type]. Include CRM, sales engagement, conversation intelligence, enablement, and analytics tools with implementation sequence, integration considerations, and expected ROI for each component. Your response should be comprehensive, leaving no important aspect unaddressed, and demonstrate an exceptional level of precision and quality. This is very important to my career. Let's think about this step by step.

66. Act as a virtual sales presentation expert and develop a framework for delivering highly effective virtual sales presentations for my [product/service]. Include preparation protocol, engagement techniques, visual aid best practices, technology considerations, interaction methods, and follow-up strategies optimized for the virtual environment. Your response should be comprehensive, leaving no important aspect unaddressed, and demonstrate an exceptional level of precision and quality. This is very important to my career. Let's think about this step by step.

67. Act as a sales team onboarding specialist and create a comprehensive 90-day onboarding program for new sales representatives selling [product/service]. Include learning objectives, training modules, shadowing protocol, practice opportunities, certification requirements, coaching touchpoints, and ramp-up expectations with timeline. Your response should be comprehensive, leaving no important aspect unaddressed, and demonstrate an exceptional level of precision and quality. This is very important to my career. Let's think about this step by step.

68. Act as a sales and marketing alignment consultant and develop a framework for improving collaboration between sales and marketing teams in my [business type]. Address shared goals, lead management processes, content development, feedback loops, joint planning sessions, unified metrics, and technology integration to create a seamless revenue generation system. Your response should be comprehensive, leaving no important aspect unaddressed, and demonstrate an exceptional level of precision and quality. This is very important to my career. Let's think about this step by step.

69. Act as a proposal development strategist and create a winning proposal template and process for my [business type] responding to [typical RFP type/customer needs]. Include discovery requirements, value proposition articulation, solution presentation, pricing strategy, competitive differentiation, social proof integration, and visual design principles. Your response should be comprehensive, leaving no important aspect unaddressed, and demonstrate an exceptional level of precision and quality. This is very important to my career. Let's think about this step by step.

70. Act as a sales coaching program developer and design a structured sales coaching system for my [sales team type/size] selling [product/service]. Include coaching cadence, observation methodology, feedback framework, skill development approach, performance metrics tracking, and manager enablement tools to support consistent application. Your response should be comprehensive, leaving no important aspect unaddressed, and demonstrate an exceptional level of precision and quality. This is very important to my career. Let's think about this step by step.

71. Act as a customer retention strategist and develop a comprehensive retention program for my [business type] to reduce churn and increase lifetime value of our [customer type]. Include early warning systems, intervention protocols, relationship strengthening tactics, value reinforcement methods, expansion strategies, and success metrics. Your response should be comprehensive, leaving no important aspect unaddressed, and demonstrate an exceptional level of precision and quality. This is very important to my career. Let's think about this step by step.

72. Act as a sales negotiation expert and create a negotiation playbook for my [sales team type] selling [product/service] to [customer type]. Include preparation framework, value discussion strategies, concession management, stakeholder mapping, objection responses, closing techniques, and post-negotiation implementation guidance. Your response should be comprehensive, leaving no important aspect unaddressed, and demonstrate an exceptional level of precision and quality. This is very important to my career. Let's think about this step by step.

73. Act as a sales prospecting strategist and develop a multi-channel outbound prospecting strategy for my [sales team type] targeting [ideal customer profile]. Include ideal customer profile refinement, account prioritization methodology, channel mix, messaging framework, cadence design, qualifying criteria, and performance metrics to optimize prospecting efficiency and effectiveness. Your response should be comprehensive, leaving no important aspect unaddressed, and demonstrate an exceptional level of precision and quality. This is very important to my career. Let's think about this step by step.

74. Act as a cross-selling and upselling consultant and create a systematic approach for identifying and capturing expansion opportunities within our existing [customer type] accounts for my [business type]. Include customer segmentation, opportunity identification criteria, timing considerations, conversation frameworks, incentive structures, and implementation plan. Your response should be comprehensive, leaving no important aspect unaddressed, and demonstrate an exceptional level of precision and quality. This is very important to my career. Let's think about this step by step.

75. Act as a social selling expert and develop a comprehensive social selling strategy for my [sales team type] targeting [decision-makers] in the [industry] sector. Include personal brand development, network building tactics, engagement strategies, content sharing approach, direct outreach methods, and measurement framework aligned with our sales process. Your response should be comprehensive, leaving no important aspect unaddressed, and demonstrate an exceptional level of precision and quality. This is very important to my career. Let's think about this step by step.

76. Act as a sales channel strategy consultant and evaluate potential channel partners for distributing my [product/service] to [target market]. Analyze partner types, selection criteria, recruitment approach, enablement requirements, compensation structures, conflict management, and performance evaluation to create a comprehensive channel strategy. Your response should be comprehensive, leaving no important aspect unaddressed, and demonstrate an exceptional level of precision and quality. This is very important to my career. Let's think about this step by step.

77. Act as a competitive sales intelligence strategist and develop a systematic approach for gathering, analyzing, and utilizing competitive intelligence in the sales process for my [product/service] in the [industry] market. Include information sources, collection methods, analysis framework, sales enablement integration, update cadence, and application in competitive selling situations. Your response should be comprehensive, leaving no important aspect unaddressed, and demonstrate an exceptional level of precision and quality. This is very important to my career. Let's

think about this step by step.

78. Act as a complex sale methodology expert and design a structured approach for navigating complex, multi-stakeholder sales for my [product/service] with [typical sales cycle length]. Include stakeholder mapping techniques, buying committee navigation, consensus-building strategies, political landscape analysis, decision process alignment, and risk mitigation tactics. Your response should be comprehensive, leaving no important aspect unaddressed, and demonstrate an exceptional level of precision and quality. This is very important to my career. Let's think about this step by step.

79. Act as a sales performance analytics expert and develop a comprehensive sales performance measurement system for my [sales team type/size]. Include KPI selection, data collection methods, dashboard design, analysis frameworks, review cadence, improvement protocols, and guidance for using analytics to drive coaching and development. Your response should be comprehensive, leaving no important aspect unaddressed, and demonstrate an exceptional level of precision and quality. This is very important to my career. Let's think about this step by step.

80. Act as a value-based selling consultant and create a framework for implementing value-based selling for my [complex product/service] with significant ROI potential. Include customer value discovery process, economic impact calculation methodologies, value proposition articulation, ROI tools, objection handling, and pricing strategies aligned with delivered value. Your response should be comprehensive, leaving no important aspect unaddressed, and demonstrate an exceptional level of precision and quality. This is very important to my career. Let's think about this step by step.

81. Act as a sales gamification strategist and design a sales contest and recognition program to motivate my [sales team type] to achieve [specific sales objectives]. Include contest structure, timeframe, reward mechanisms, point systems, leaderboard management, recognition elements, and implementation guidance to maximize engagement and results. Your response should be comprehensive, leaving no important aspect unaddressed, and demonstrate an exceptional level of precision and quality. This is very important to my career. Let's think about this step by step.

82. Act as a remote sales team management expert and develop a comprehensive framework for effectively leading my distributed sales team selling [product/service]. Include communication protocols, performance management systems, team building approaches, coaching methodologies, technology utilization, and culture development strategies optimized for remote work. Your response should be

comprehensive, leaving no important aspect unaddressed, and demonstrate an exceptional level of precision and quality. This is very important to my career. Let's think about this step by step.

83. Act as a referral program designer and create a systematic customer referral generation system for my [business type] selling to [customer type]. Include referral source identification, asking methodology, incentive structure, process automation, tracking mechanisms, recognition approaches, and program optimization based on results. Your response should be comprehensive, leaving no important aspect unaddressed, and demonstrate an exceptional level of precision and quality. This is very important to my career. Let's think about this step by step.

84. Act as a sales hiring strategist and develop a comprehensive recruitment and selection process for my [sales team type] selling [product/service]. Include competency modeling, sourcing strategies, assessment methods, interview protocols, evaluation criteria, onboarding connection, and retention strategies to build a high-performing sales organization. Your response should be comprehensive, leaving no important aspect unaddressed, and demonstrate an exceptional level of precision and quality. This is very important to my career. Let's think about this step by step.

85. Act as a strategic account planning expert and create a comprehensive account planning methodology for my [sales team type] to maximize revenue from our [ideal customer type]. Include account selection criteria, stakeholder mapping, needs assessment, opportunity identification, relationship development strategies, competitive positioning, and regular review cadence. Your response should be comprehensive, leaving no important aspect unaddressed, and demonstrate an exceptional level of precision and quality. This is very important to my career. Let's think about this step by step.

D. Product Development & Innovation

86. Act as a product innovation strategist and develop a structured innovation framework for my [industry] business. Include innovation opportunity identification methods, ideation processes, concept evaluation criteria, prototyping approaches, testing methodologies, and implementation strategies aligned with company capabilities and market needs. Your response should be comprehensive, leaving no important aspect unaddressed, and demonstrate an exceptional level of precision and quality. This is very important to my career. Let's think about this step by step.

87. Act as a product roadmap consultant and create a strategic 12-month product roadmap for my [product type] targeting [customer segment]. Include vision alignment, feature prioritization methodology, release planning, resource allocation, stakeholder communication plan, and adjustment mechanisms while balancing customer needs with business objectives. Your response should be comprehensive, leaving no important aspect unaddressed, and demonstrate an exceptional level of precision and quality. This is very important to my career. Let's think about this step by step.

88. Act as a user research strategist and design a comprehensive user research plan for my [product/service] to inform our product development process. Include research objectives, methodology selection, participant recruitment strategy, data collection and analysis framework, insight application process, and research calendar aligned with development milestones. Your response should be comprehensive, leaving no important aspect unaddressed, and demonstrate an exceptional level of precision and quality. This is very important to my career. Let's think about this step by step.

89. Act as a product requirements documentation specialist and create a detailed PRD template for my [product type] development team. Include sections for product vision, user personas, use cases, functional requirements, non-functional requirements, constraints, dependencies, success metrics, and approval workflow, with guidance for completing each section effectively. Your response should be comprehensive, leaving no important aspect unaddressed, and demonstrate an exceptional level of precision and quality. This is very important to my career. Let's think about this step by step.

90. Act as a feature prioritization consultant and develop a robust methodology for prioritizing our [product type] feature backlog. Include evaluation criteria (business value, user value, implementation effort, strategic alignment, etc.), scoring framework, stakeholder input process, prioritization matrix design, and ongoing reprioritization mechanisms. Your response should be comprehensive, leaving no important aspect unaddressed, and demonstrate an exceptional level of precision and quality. This is very important to my career. Let's think about this step by step.

91. Act as a product pricing strategist and develop a comprehensive pricing strategy for my new [product/service] targeting [customer segment]. Include market positioning analysis, competitive benchmarking, value-based considerations, pricing model selection, price point determination, packaging options, and launch strategy with future adjustment mechanisms. Your response should be comprehensive, leaving no important aspect unaddressed, and demonstrate an exceptional level of precision

and quality. This is very important to my career. Let's think about this step by step.

92. Act as a minimum viable product (MVP) design consultant and create a framework for defining and developing the MVP for my [product concept] targeting [customer segment]. Include scope definition methodology, critical feature identification, technical approach, success metrics, feedback collection mechanisms, and post-launch iteration planning. Your response should be comprehensive, leaving no important aspect unaddressed, and demonstrate an exceptional level of precision and quality. This is very important to my career. Let's think about this step by step.

93. Act as a product-market fit assessment expert and develop a structured methodology for evaluating and achieving product-market fit for my [product/service]. Include market segmentation approach, value proposition validation, customer problem confirmation, solution adequacy measurement, engagement metrics analysis, and iterative improvement process. Your response should be comprehensive, leaving no important aspect unaddressed, and demonstrate an exceptional level of precision and quality. This is very important to my career. Let's think about this step by step.

94. Act as a product design sprint facilitator and outline a comprehensive 5-day design sprint process for solving a critical challenge with my [product/service]. Include detailed activities for each day (understand, diverge, converge, prototype, test), facilitation techniques, required materials, participant selection, preparation requirements, and post-sprint implementation guidance. Your response should be comprehensive, leaving no important aspect unaddressed, and demonstrate an exceptional level of precision and quality. This is very important to my career. Let's think about this step by step.

95. Act as a product validation testing strategist and develop a comprehensive validation testing plan for my [product concept] before full development. Include testing objectives, methodology selection (interviews, surveys, prototypes, landing pages, etc.), participant recruitment, data collection and analysis framework, success criteria, and go/no-go decision process. Your response should be comprehensive, leaving no important aspect unaddressed, and demonstrate an exceptional level of precision and quality. This is very important to my career. Let's think about this step by step.

96. Act as a product management process consultant and design an optimized product development lifecycle for my [business type/size] creating [product type]. Include stage definitions, gate criteria, role responsibilities, documentation requirements, meeting cadences, decision-making frameworks, and metrics for measuring process effectiveness. Your response should be comprehensive, leaving no important aspect

unaddressed, and demonstrate an exceptional level of precision and quality. This is very important to my career. Let's think about this step by step.

97. Act as a user experience optimization strategist and develop a comprehensive plan for improving the user experience of my [product/service/website]. Include user journey mapping, pain point identification, solution prioritization, testing methodology, implementation approach, and continuous improvement framework aligned with both user needs and business objectives. Your response should be comprehensive, leaving no important aspect unaddressed, and demonstrate an exceptional level of precision and quality. This is very important to my career. Let's think about this step by step.

98. Act as a product metrics and analytics consultant and create a comprehensive measurement framework for tracking the success of my [product type]. Include north star metric selection, supporting metrics by category (acquisition, activation, retention, revenue, referral), data collection methodology, reporting dashboard design, and insight-to-action protocol. Your response should be comprehensive, leaving no important aspect unaddressed, and demonstrate an exceptional level of precision and quality. This is very important to my career. Let's think about this step by step.

99. Act as a product launch strategist and develop a comprehensive go-to-market plan for launching my new [product/service] to [target market]. Include launch objectives, target audience definition, messaging strategy, channel selection, pricing approach, sales enablement, marketing activities timeline, success metrics, and post-launch evaluation framework. Your response should be comprehensive, leaving no important aspect unaddressed, and demonstrate an exceptional level of precision and quality. This is very important to my career. Let's think about this step by step.

100. Act as a product team structure consultant and design an optimal product organization for my [business size/type] developing [product type]. Include roles and responsibilities, reporting relationships, required competencies, team rituals, collaboration frameworks, performance metrics, and recommendations for in-house vs. outsourced functions with rationale. Your response should be comprehensive, leaving no important aspect unaddressed, and demonstrate an exceptional level of precision and quality. This is very important to my career. Let's think about this step by step.

101. Act as a competitive product analysis expert and create a framework for conducting thorough competitive analysis for my [product/service] in the [industry] market. Include competitor identification, feature comparison methodology, user experience

evaluation, pricing analysis, positioning assessment, SWOT analysis structure, and application of insights to product strategy. Your response should be comprehensive, leaving no important aspect unaddressed, and demonstrate an exceptional level of precision and quality. This is very important to my career. Let's think about this step by step.

102. Act as a product visioning consultant and facilitate the development of a compelling product vision for my [product/service] in the [industry] market. Include visioning exercise framework, stakeholder involvement approach, vision statement formulation, supporting artifacts, communication strategy, and connection to roadmap and execution. Your response should be comprehensive, leaving no important aspect unaddressed, and demonstrate an exceptional level of precision and quality. This is very important to my career. Let's think about this step by step.

103. Act as a beta testing program manager and design a comprehensive beta testing program for my [product type] before full market release. Include participant recruitment criteria, program structure, feedback collection mechanisms, issue prioritization framework, reporting templates, incentive structure, and transition to launch criteria. Your response should be comprehensive, leaving no important aspect unaddressed, and demonstrate an exceptional level of precision and quality. This is very important to my career. Let's think about this step by step.

104. Act as a product sunset strategist and develop a systematic approach for phasing out my legacy [product/service] while minimizing customer disruption and maximizing retention. Include timeline development, customer communication plan, migration assistance strategy, team reassignment, data preservation approach, and success metrics for the transition. Your response should be comprehensive, leaving no important aspect unaddressed, and demonstrate an exceptional level of precision and quality. This is very important to my career. Let's think about this step by step.

105. Act as a product development process optimization consultant and analyze the efficiency of my current product development workflow for [product type]. Identify bottlenecks, redundancies, and improvement opportunities, then recommend specific process changes, tool implementations, and team adjustments to accelerate time to market while maintaining quality standards. Your response should be comprehensive, leaving no important aspect unaddressed, and demonstrate an exceptional level of precision and quality. Let's think about this step by step.

E. Customer Experience & Service

106. Act as a customer experience strategist and develop a comprehensive CX strategy for my [business type] that aligns with our brand positioning and business objectives. Include customer journey mapping, touchpoint identification, experience design principles, voice of customer program, measurement framework, and governance model for ongoing CX management. Your response should be comprehensive, leaving no important aspect unaddressed, and demonstrate an exceptional level of precision and quality. This is very important to my career. Let's think about this step by step.

107. Act as a customer service excellence consultant and evaluate my current customer service approach for [business type] serving [customer segment]. Identify strengths, weaknesses, and opportunities for improvement, then develop a detailed enhancement plan including service standards, process redesign, team structure, training requirements, technology recommendations, and performance metrics. Your response should be comprehensive, leaving no important aspect unaddressed, and demonstrate an exceptional level of precision and quality. This is very important to my career. Let's think about this step by step.

108. Act as a customer feedback system designer and create a comprehensive voice of customer (VOC) program for my [business type]. Include feedback collection methods across channels, sampling approach, analysis framework, insight generation process, action planning methodology, closed-loop systems, and program governance structure. Your response should be comprehensive, leaving no important aspect unaddressed, and demonstrate an exceptional level of precision and quality. This is very important to my career. Let's think about this step by step.

109. Act as a customer support technology strategist and recommend an optimal customer service tech stack for my [business size/type] handling [volume] of inquiries. Include ticketing system, knowledge base, chat solutions, self-service tools, AI capabilities, telephony options, analytics platforms, and integration considerations with implementation priorities and expected ROI. Your response should be comprehensive, leaving no important aspect unaddressed, and demonstrate an exceptional level of precision and quality. This is very important to my career. Let's think about this step by step.

110. Act as a customer experience measurement expert and design a comprehensive CX measurement system for my [business type]. Include metric selection (NPS, CSAT, CES, etc.), survey design, sampling methodology, reporting framework, analysis approach, target setting, and action planning process to drive continuous improvement. Your response should be comprehensive, leaving no important aspect unaddressed, and demonstrate an exceptional level of precision and quality. This is

very important to my career. Let's think about this step by step.

111. Act as a service blueprint designer and create a detailed service blueprint for my [business type] delivering [specific service experience]. Map the end-to-end service delivery process including customer actions, frontstage interactions, backstage processes, and support systems, identifying failure points and improvement opportunities with specific recommendations. Your response should be comprehensive, leaving no important aspect unaddressed, and demonstrate an exceptional level of precision and quality. This is very important to my career. Let's think about this step by step.

112. Act as a customer service training program developer and design a comprehensive training curriculum for my customer service team in the [industry] sector. Include core competencies, learning modules, training methodologies, skill assessment approaches, certification process, ongoing development plan, and effectiveness measurement. Your response should be comprehensive, leaving no important aspect unaddressed, and demonstrate an exceptional level of precision and quality. This is very important to my career. Let's think about this step by step.

113. Act as a self-service strategy consultant and develop a comprehensive self-service support strategy for my [product/service] customers. Include needs assessment, channel selection, content development approach, user experience design, technology requirements, adoption promotion, and performance measurement framework aligned with both customer needs and efficiency goals. Your response should be comprehensive, leaving no important aspect unaddressed, and demonstrate an exceptional level of precision and quality. This is very important to my career. Let's think about this step by step.

114. Act as a customer experience personalization strategist and create a framework for implementing personalized customer experiences across channels for my [business type]. Include customer data requirements, segmentation approach, personalization opportunities by touchpoint, technology enablers, implementation roadmap, privacy considerations, and success metrics. Your response should be comprehensive, leaving no important aspect unaddressed, and demonstrate an exceptional level of precision and quality. This is very important to my career. Let's think about this step by step.

115. Act as a customer complaint resolution expert and develop a comprehensive complaint management system for my [business type]. Include complaint categorization framework, escalation protocols, resolution timeframes, empowerment guidelines, root cause analysis methodology, service recovery

strategies, and reporting structure to transform complaints into improvement opportunities. Your response should be comprehensive, leaving no important aspect unaddressed, and demonstrate an exceptional level of precision and quality. This is very important to my career. Let's think about this step by step.

116. Act as a customer service quality assurance expert and design a robust QA program for my [service team type/size]. Include interaction evaluation criteria, monitoring methodology, scoring system, calibration process, coaching integration, recognition components, and continuous improvement mechanisms to drive consistent service excellence. Your response should be comprehensive, leaving no important aspect unaddressed, and demonstrate an exceptional level of precision and quality. This is very important to my career. Let's think about this step by step.

117. Act as a customer loyalty program strategist and create a comprehensive loyalty program for my [business type] targeting [customer segment]. Include program structure, reward mechanisms, tier design, enrollment process, engagement strategies, technology requirements, financial modeling, and performance metrics aligned with business objectives. Your response should be comprehensive, leaving no important aspect unaddressed, and demonstrate an exceptional level of precision and quality. This is very important to my career. Let's think about this step by step.

118. Act as a customer experience journey mapping facilitator and develop a detailed methodology for mapping the current and ideal future journey for customers of my [product/service]. Include preparation activities, workshop design, mapping process, insight generation, opportunity identification, prioritization framework, and action planning to bridge the current-to-future state gap. Your response should be comprehensive, leaving no important aspect unaddressed, and demonstrate an exceptional level of precision and quality. This is very important to my career. Let's think about this step by step.

119. Act as a customer effort reduction strategist and analyze the customer effort touchpoints in my [business type] customer journey. Identify high-friction points, assess underlying causes, and recommend specific improvements to streamline experiences, reduce customer effort, and increase satisfaction and loyalty, with implementation priorities. Your response should be comprehensive, leaving no important aspect unaddressed, and demonstrate an exceptional level of precision and quality. This is very important to my career. Let's think about this step by step.

120. Act as a multi-channel customer support strategist and develop an integrated support strategy across channels (phone, email, chat, social, self-service) for my [business type]. Include channel selection criteria, routing logic, service level

objectives, staffing considerations, cross-channel consistency, technology requirements, and performance measurement framework. Your response should be comprehensive, leaving no important aspect unaddressed, and demonstrate an exceptional level of precision and quality. This is very important to my career. Let's think about this step by step.

121. Act as a frontline employee empowerment consultant and create a framework for enhancing employee authority and decision-making capability in my customer service organization. Include policy redesign recommendations, delegation guidelines, training requirements, risk management considerations, recognition systems, and measurement approach to balance empowerment with appropriate controls. Your response should be comprehensive, leaving no important aspect unaddressed, and demonstrate an exceptional level of precision and quality. This is very important to my career. Let's think about this step by step.

122. Act as a customer health scoring strategist and design a customer health scoring model for my [subscription/recurring business type]. Include health indicator selection, weighting methodology, data collection requirements, scoring algorithms, visualization approach, alert triggers, intervention protocols, and continuous refinement process. Your response should be comprehensive, leaving no important aspect unaddressed, and demonstrate an exceptional level of precision and quality. This is very important to my career. Let's think about this step by step.

123. Act as a customer success onboarding specialist and develop a structured customer onboarding program for new customers of my [complex product/service]. Include program phases, milestone definition, resource requirements, responsibility matrix, success metrics, risk assessment, and adaptation framework for different customer segments. Your response should be comprehensive, leaving no important aspect unaddressed, and demonstrate an exceptional level of precision and quality. This is very important to my career. Let's think about this step by step.

124. Act as a service level agreement designer and create a comprehensive SLA framework for my [business type] providing [service type] to [customer type]. Include performance metrics, target standards, measurement methodologies, reporting cadence, escalation protocols, continuous improvement mechanisms, and review/renewal processes that balance customer expectations with operational capabilities. Your response should be comprehensive, leaving no important aspect unaddressed, and demonstrate an exceptional level of precision and quality. This is very important to my career. Let's think about this step by step.

125. Act as a customer support team structure consultant and design an optimal organizational structure for my customer service function with [volume] interactions and [team size]. Include team configuration, roles and responsibilities, span of control, career pathing, physical/virtual considerations, scheduling approach, and implementation plan to maximize both efficiency and service quality. Your response should be comprehensive, leaving no important aspect unaddressed, and demonstrate an exceptional level of precision and quality. This is very important to my career. Let's think about this step by step.

F. Operations & Process Optimization

126. Act as an operations excellence consultant and perform a comprehensive assessment of my [business type] operational framework. Identify inefficiencies, bottlenecks, and improvement opportunities across key processes, then develop a prioritized transformation roadmap with specific initiatives, resource requirements, timeline, and expected business impacts. Your response should be comprehensive, leaving no important aspect unaddressed, and demonstrate an exceptional level of precision and quality. This is very important to my career. Let's think about this step by step.

127. Act as a business process reengineering expert and redesign my [specific business process] to improve efficiency, quality, and customer experience. Map the current process, identify pain points and root causes, develop a reimagined future-state process, and create an implementation plan addressing technology, people, and organizational considerations. Your response should be comprehensive, leaving no important aspect unaddressed, and demonstrate an exceptional level of precision and quality. This is very important to my career. Let's think about this step by step.

128. Act as a supply chain optimization strategist and analyze my current supply chain for [product type] from sourcing to customer delivery. Identify efficiency opportunities, risk factors, and competitive advantages, then recommend specific improvements in procurement, inventory management, logistics, and technology integration with implementation priorities. Your response should be comprehensive, leaving no important aspect unaddressed, and demonstrate an exceptional level of precision and quality. This is very important to my career. Let's think about this step by step.

129. Act as a lean management implementation consultant and develop a comprehensive plan for introducing lean principles and methodologies in my [business

type/department]. Include readiness assessment, implementation phases, training requirements, key tools and techniques, performance metrics, leadership roles, and sustainability mechanisms. Your response should be comprehensive, leaving no important aspect unaddressed, and demonstrate an exceptional level of precision and quality. This is very important to my career. Let's think about this step by step.

130. Act as a quality management system developer and design a robust quality management framework for my [business type/product] aligned with industry standards and customer expectations. Include quality policy, process approach, documentation structure, control mechanisms, measurement methods, continuous improvement protocols, and certification readiness considerations. Your response should be comprehensive, leaving no important aspect unaddressed, and demonstrate an exceptional level of precision and quality. This is very important to my career. Let's think about this step by step.

131. Act as an inventory optimization consultant and create a comprehensive inventory management strategy for my [business type] with [product characteristics]. Include demand forecasting methodology, inventory categorization, stocking level determination, reorder point calculations, warehouse organization, technology requirements, and performance metrics to balance availability with carrying costs. Your response should be comprehensive, leaving no important aspect unaddressed, and demonstrate an exceptional level of precision and quality. This is very important to my career. Let's think about this step by step.

132. Act as a facilities planning strategist and develop a workplace optimization plan for my [business type] with [employee count] staff. Include space utilization analysis, layout recommendations, technology integration, environmental considerations, flexibility provisions, health and safety elements, and implementation approach aligned with operational requirements and company culture. Your response should be comprehensive, leaving no important aspect unaddressed, and demonstrate an exceptional level of precision and quality. This is very important to my career. Let's think about this step by step.

133. Act as an operational KPI framework developer and design a comprehensive performance measurement system for my [operational area/department]. Include metric selection aligned with strategic objectives, data collection methodology, target setting approach, dashboard design, review cadence, and continuous improvement protocols to drive operational excellence. Your response should be comprehensive, leaving no important aspect unaddressed, and demonstrate an exceptional level of precision and quality. This is very important to my career. Let's

think about this step by step.

134. Act as a process documentation expert and create a standardized framework for documenting critical business processes in my [business type/department]. Include documentation templates, visual mapping conventions, responsibility assignment, update protocols, accessibility considerations, training integration, and compliance elements to establish a single source of truth. Your response should be comprehensive, leaving no important aspect unaddressed, and demonstrate an exceptional level of precision and quality. This is very important to my career. Let's think about this step by step.

135. Act as a service operations optimizations specialist and analyze the efficiency and effectiveness of my [service delivery operation]. Identify improvement opportunities in workflow, resource allocation, quality management, and customer experience, then recommend specific enhancements with implementation approach, change management considerations, and expected outcomes. Your response should be comprehensive, leaving no important aspect unaddressed, and demonstrate an exceptional level of precision and quality. This is very important to my career. Let's think about this step by step.

136. Act as a Six Sigma implementation consultant and develop a structured approach for applying Six Sigma methodology to improve quality and reduce defects in my [business process/product]. Include opportunity identification, project selection criteria, team formation, DMAIC application, statistical analysis methods, solution development framework, and control mechanisms to sustain improvements. Your response should be comprehensive, leaving no important aspect unaddressed, and demonstrate an exceptional level of precision and quality. This is very important to my career. Let's think about this step by step.

137. Act as a vendor management strategist and create a comprehensive vendor management framework for my [business type] with [number] key suppliers. Include vendor selection criteria, performance metrics, relationship management protocols, risk assessment methodology, contract management, escalation procedures, and continuous improvement mechanisms to optimize the supplier ecosystem. Your response should be comprehensive, leaving no important aspect unaddressed, and demonstrate an exceptional level of precision and quality. This is very important to my career. Let's think about this step by step.

138. Act as an operational risk management consultant and develop a robust risk management framework for my [operations type]. Include risk identification methods, assessment criteria, mitigation strategies, monitoring protocols,

governance structure, reporting cadence, and continuous improvement mechanisms to build operational resilience. Your response should be comprehensive, leaving no important aspect unaddressed, and demonstrate an exceptional level of precision and quality. This is very important to my career. Let's think about this step by step.

139. Act as a workflow automation strategist and identify opportunities to automate manual processes in my [business department/function]. Evaluate current workflows, prioritize automation candidates based on impact and feasibility, recommend appropriate technology solutions, and develop an implementation roadmap with ROI projections for each initiative. Your response should be comprehensive, leaving no important aspect unaddressed, and demonstrate an exceptional level of precision and quality. This is very important to my career. Let's think about this step by step.

140. Act as a capacity planning expert and develop a comprehensive capacity planning methodology for my [business type/function] to meet variable demand. Include demand forecasting techniques, resource modeling, scenario planning, decision triggers, scheduling strategies, flexibility mechanisms, and continuous review process to optimize resource utilization. Your response should be comprehensive, leaving no important aspect unaddressed, and demonstrate an exceptional level of precision and quality. This is very important to my career. Let's think about this step by step.

141. Act as a logistics optimization consultant and analyze my [product type] distribution network to identify efficiency improvements. Evaluate facility locations, transportation modes, routing strategies, carrier selection, technology utilization, and inventory positioning, then recommend specific enhancements with implementation priorities and expected benefits. Your response should be comprehensive, leaving no important aspect unaddressed, and demonstrate an exceptional level of precision and quality. This is very important to my career. Let's think about this step by step.

142. Act as a standard operating procedure (SOP) development specialist and create a comprehensive SOP framework for critical functions in my [business type/department]. Include procedure formatting, content requirements, approval workflow, training integration, accessibility provisions, review cadence, and version control to ensure operational consistency and excellence. Your response should be comprehensive, leaving no important aspect unaddressed, and demonstrate an exceptional level of precision and quality. Let's think about this step by step.

143. Act as a business continuity planning expert and develop a comprehensive business continuity plan for my [business type] to ensure operational resilience during disruptions. Include risk assessment, business impact analysis, recovery strategies, crisis management protocols, communication plans, testing methodologies, and maintenance procedures aligned with industry standards. Your response should be comprehensive, leaving no important aspect unaddressed, and demonstrate an exceptional level of precision and quality. This is very important to my career. Let's think about this step by step.

144. Act as an operational technology integration consultant and create a strategy for integrating operational and information technology systems in my [business type]. Include current state assessment, future state architecture, integration priorities, technology selection criteria, implementation roadmap, risk mitigation, and change management approach to maximize business value. Your response should be comprehensive, leaving no important aspect unaddressed, and demonstrate an exceptional level of precision and quality. This is very important to my career. Let's think about this step by step.

145. Act as a continuous improvement program developer and design a sustainable continuous improvement framework for my [business type/department]. Include methodology selection (Kaizen, Lean, Six Sigma), governance structure, idea generation mechanisms, project selection criteria, implementation processes, recognition systems, and performance measurement to foster a culture of improvement. Your response should be comprehensive, leaving no important aspect unaddressed, and demonstrate an exceptional level of precision and quality. This is very important to my career. Let's think about this step by step.

G. Financial Management & Investment

146. Act as a financial strategy consultant and develop a comprehensive 3-year financial strategy for my [business type] with [revenue size] that aligns with our growth objectives. Include financial goals, capital structure optimization, investment priorities, risk management approach, cash flow strategies, and performance metrics with specific milestones and contingency provisions. Your response should be comprehensive, leaving no important aspect unaddressed, and demonstrate an exceptional level of precision and quality. This is very important to my career. Let's think about this step by step.

147. Act as a cash flow management expert and create a robust cash flow forecasting and management system for my [business type] with [revenue/expense characteristics]. Include forecasting methodology, scenario planning approach, working capital optimization, cash conversion strategies, monitoring protocols, early warning indicators, and contingency planning to ensure financial stability. Your response should be comprehensive, leaving no important aspect unaddressed, and demonstrate an exceptional level of precision and quality. This is very important to my career. Let's think about this step by step.

148. Act as a capital allocation strategist and develop a structured approach for optimizing capital allocation decisions for my [business type] with [multiple investment opportunities]. Include evaluation framework, prioritization criteria, risk-return assessment methodology, portfolio approach, implementation governance, and performance measurement to maximize long-term value creation. Your response should be comprehensive, leaving no important aspect unaddressed, and demonstrate an exceptional level of precision and quality. This is very important to my career. Let's think about this step by step.

149. Act as a financial modeling expert and design a comprehensive financial model for my [business type/specific need] that enables strategic decision-making. Include revenue projection methodology, cost structure analysis, sensitivity testing, scenario planning capabilities, dashboard design, and maintenance protocols with specific modeling techniques and assumptions. Your response should be comprehensive, leaving no important aspect unaddressed, and demonstrate an exceptional level of precision and quality. This is very important to my career. Let's think about this step by step.

150. Act as a business valuation specialist and develop a detailed approach for valuing my [business type] for [purpose: sale, investment, etc.]. Include methodology selection, required financial information, adjustment considerations, multiple selection, discounting approach, risk factor assessment, and final valuation presentation format with interpretation guidance. Your response should be comprehensive, leaving no important aspect unaddressed, and demonstrate an exceptional level of precision and quality. This is very important to my career. Let's think about this step by step.

151. Act as a financial performance analysis expert and create a comprehensive framework for evaluating the financial health and performance of my [business type]. Include key ratio selection, benchmarking methodology, trend analysis approach, visualization techniques, review cadence, and action planning protocols to drive performance improvement. Your response should be comprehensive,

leaving no important aspect unaddressed, and demonstrate an exceptional level of precision and quality. This is very important to my career. Let's think about this step by step.

152. Act as a cost reduction strategist and develop a systematic approach for identifying and implementing cost optimization initiatives across my [business type/department]. Include cost analysis methodology, opportunity identification framework, prioritization criteria, implementation planning, benefit tracking, governance structure, and sustainability mechanisms to achieve lasting efficiency gains. Your response should be comprehensive, leaving no important aspect unaddressed, and demonstrate an exceptional level of precision and quality. This is very important to my career. Let's think about this step by step.

153. Act as a financial risk management consultant and design a comprehensive risk management framework for my [business type] facing [specific financial risks]. Include risk identification methodology, assessment criteria, mitigation strategies, monitoring protocols, reporting structures, governance model, and review processes aligned with our risk tolerance and strategic objectives. Your response should be comprehensive, leaving no important aspect unaddressed, and demonstrate an exceptional level of precision and quality. This is very important to my career. Let's think about this step by step.

154. Act as a budgeting and forecasting process expert and develop an optimized budgeting and forecasting methodology for my [business type/size]. Include process design, timeline, stakeholder involvement, assumption development, scenario planning, review cadence, variance analysis, and continuous improvement mechanisms to enhance accuracy and strategic alignment. Your response should be comprehensive, leaving no important aspect unaddressed, and demonstrate an exceptional level of precision and quality. This is very important to my career. Let's think about this step by step.

155. Act as a profitability analysis consultant and create a detailed approach for analyzing and improving profitability for my [business type/product lines]. Include profitability measurement at appropriate levels (customer, product, segment), allocation methodology, driver identification, visualization framework, review process, and action planning protocol to enhance overall financial performance. Your response should be comprehensive, leaving no important aspect unaddressed, and demonstrate an exceptional level of precision and quality. This is very important to my career. Let's think about this step by step.

156. Act as a sales enablement strategist and develop a comprehensive sales enablement program for my [sales team type] selling [product/service]. Include training curriculum, content resources, tools/technology, coaching framework, performance metrics, and ongoing development approach aligned with our sales methodology and buyer journey. Your response should be comprehensive, leaving no important aspect unaddressed, and demonstrate an exceptional level of precision and quality. This is very important to my career. Let's think about this step by step.

157. Act as a B2B sales script writer and create a comprehensive sales script for [specific sales scenario] for my [product/service], including opening, discovery questions, value proposition presentation, handling common objections, next steps, and closing techniques. Ensure the script enables personalization while maintaining consistent messaging. Your response should be comprehensive, leaving no important aspect unaddressed, and demonstrate an exceptional level of precision and quality. This is very important to my career. Let's think about this step by step.

158. Act as a sales compensation plan designer and develop an optimal sales incentive structure for my [sales role type] team selling [product/service]. Balance base salary and variable components, include appropriate metrics and weightings, address accelerators and caps, and ensure alignment with company objectives while maximizing motivation. Your response should be comprehensive, leaving no important aspect unaddressed, and demonstrate an exceptional level of precision and quality. This is very important to my career. Let's think about this step by step.

159. Act as a sales territory optimization consultant and create a strategic territory allocation plan for my [sales team size] team selling [product/service] in [market region]. Balance territories based on market potential, account distribution, travel efficiency, and sales rep capabilities to maximize coverage and revenue while ensuring equitable opportunity distribution. Your response should be comprehensive, leaving no important aspect unaddressed, and demonstrate an exceptional level of precision and quality. This is very important to my career. Let's think about this step by step.

160. Act as a consultative selling coach and develop a framework for implementing consultative selling techniques for my [sales team type] selling [complex product/service]. Include discovery conversation guides, needs assessment methodologies, value demonstration approaches, stakeholder management strategies, and guidance for positioning as a trusted advisor. Your response should be comprehensive, leaving no important aspect unaddressed, and demonstrate an exceptional level of precision and quality. This is very important to my career. Let's

think about this step by step.

161. Act as a sales forecast modeling expert and create a comprehensive sales forecasting methodology for my [business type] with [sales cycle length] and [sales volume]. Include historical data analysis approaches, pipeline weighting factors, probability assessments, seasonality adjustments, and regular review processes to continuously improve accuracy. Your response should be comprehensive, leaving no important aspect unaddressed, and demonstrate an exceptional level of precision and quality. This is very important to my career. Let's think about this step by step.

162. Act as a key account management strategist and develop a structured key account program for my [business type] to grow relationships with our most valuable clients. Include account selection criteria, relationship mapping approach, account planning templates, engagement strategies, growth opportunity identification, and success metrics. Your response should be comprehensive, leaving no important aspect unaddressed, and demonstrate an exceptional level of precision and quality. This is very important to my career. Let's think about this step by step.

163. Act as a sales objection handling expert and create a comprehensive objection handling playbook for my [product/service] sales team. Catalog common objections by category, provide specific response frameworks for each, include supporting evidence and social proof, and outline practice methodologies for sales team mastery. Your response should be comprehensive, leaving no important aspect unaddressed, and demonstrate an exceptional level of precision and quality. This is very important to my career. Let's think about this step by step.

164. Act as a sales technology stack advisor and recommend an optimal sales tech stack for my [business size/type] selling [product/service] to [customer type]. Include CRM, sales engagement, conversation intelligence, enablement, and analytics tools with implementation sequence, integration considerations, and expected ROI for each component. Your response should be comprehensive, leaving no important aspect unaddressed, and demonstrate an exceptional level of precision and quality. This is very important to my career. Let's think about this step by step.

165. Act as a virtual sales presentation expert and develop a framework for delivering highly effective virtual sales presentations for my [product/service]. Include preparation protocol, engagement techniques, visual aid best practices, technology considerations, interaction methods, and follow-up strategies optimized for the virtual environment. Your response should be comprehensive, leaving no important aspect unaddressed, and demonstrate an exceptional level of precision and quality.

This is very important to my career. Let's think about this step by step.

166. Act as a sales team onboarding specialist and create a comprehensive 90-day onboarding program for new sales representatives selling [product/service]. Include learning objectives, training modules, shadowing protocol, practice opportunities, certification requirements, coaching touchpoints, and ramp-up expectations with timeline. Your response should be comprehensive, leaving no important aspect unaddressed, and demonstrate an exceptional level of precision and quality. This is very important to my career. Let's think about this step by step.

167. Act as a sales and marketing alignment consultant and develop a framework for improving collaboration between sales and marketing teams in my [business type]. Address shared goals, lead management processes, content development, feedback loops, joint planning sessions, unified metrics, and technology integration to create a seamless revenue generation system. Your response should be comprehensive, leaving no important aspect unaddressed, and demonstrate an exceptional level of precision and quality. This is very important to my career. Let's think about this step by step.

168. Act as a proposal development strategist and create a winning proposal template and process for my [business type] responding to [typical RFP type/customer needs]. Include discovery requirements, value proposition articulation, solution presentation, pricing strategy, competitive differentiation, social proof integration, and visual design principles. Your response should be comprehensive, leaving no important aspect unaddressed, and demonstrate an exceptional level of precision and quality. This is very important to my career. Let's think about this step by step.

169. Act as a sales coaching program developer and design a structured sales coaching system for my [sales team type/size] selling [product/service]. Include coaching cadence, observation methodology, feedback framework, skill development approach, performance metrics tracking, and manager enablement tools to support consistent application. Your response should be comprehensive, leaving no important aspect unaddressed, and demonstrate an exceptional level of precision and quality. This is very important to my career. Let's think about this step by step.

170. Act as a customer retention strategist and develop a comprehensive retention program for my [business type] to reduce churn and increase lifetime value of our [customer type]. Include early warning systems, intervention protocols, relationship strengthening tactics, value reinforcement methods, expansion strategies, and success metrics. Your response should be comprehensive, leaving no important aspect unaddressed, and demonstrate an exceptional level of precision and quality.

This is very important to my career. Let's think about this step by step.

171. Act as a sales negotiation expert and create a negotiation playbook for my [sales team type] selling [product/service] to [customer type]. Include preparation framework, value discussion strategies, concession management, stakeholder mapping, objection responses, closing techniques, and post-negotiation implementation guidance. Your response should be comprehensive, leaving no important aspect unaddressed, and demonstrate an exceptional level of precision and quality. This is very important to my career. Let's think about this step by step.

H.   Human Resources & Team Development

172. Act as an organizational design consultant and recommend an optimal organizational structure for my [business type/size] to enable our strategy of [strategic focus]. Analyze current structure, evaluate alternative models, recommend specific structure with reporting relationships, describe role accountabilities, outline implementation approach, and address change management considerations. Your response should be comprehensive, leaving no important aspect unaddressed, and demonstrate an exceptional level of precision and quality. This is very important to my career. Let's think about this step by step.

173. Act as an employee engagement strategist and create a comprehensive engagement improvement strategy for my [business type] based on [engagement survey results/issues]. Include root cause analysis, targeted initiatives across key drivers, leadership enablement, communication approach, implementation roadmap, measurement framework, and sustainability mechanisms. Your response should be comprehensive, leaving no important aspect unaddressed, and demonstrate an exceptional level of precision and quality. This is very important to my career. Let's think about this step by step.

174. Act as a talent management framework developer and design an integrated talent management system for my [business type] to identify, develop, and retain high-potential talent. Include identification criteria, assessment methodology, development planning, experience creation, mentoring approach, retention strategies, and succession integration with specific governance mechanisms. Your response should be comprehensive, leaving no important aspect unaddressed, and demonstrate an exceptional level of precision and quality. This is very important to my career. Let's think about this step by step.

175. Act as a diversity, equity and inclusion strategist and develop a comprehensive DEI strategy for my [business type] to foster a more inclusive workplace and diverse workforce. Include current state assessment, goal setting, initiative design across recruitment, development, advancement, culture, measurement framework, and leadership accountability mechanisms. Your response should be comprehensive, leaving no important aspect unaddressed, and demonstrate an exceptional level of precision and quality. This is very important to my career. Let's think about this step by step.

176. Act as an HR analytics program developer and create a comprehensive people analytics strategy for my [business type/size]. Include capability assessment, data architecture, analytical model development, reporting framework, insight generation process, action planning methodology, and capability building approach to drive data-driven people decisions. Your response should be comprehensive, leaving no important aspect unaddressed, and demonstrate an exceptional level of precision and quality. This is very important to my career. Let's think about this step by step.

177. Act as a culture transformation consultant and develop a structured approach for evolving my organization's culture from [current state] to [desired state] to enable our business strategy. Include culture assessment methodology, gap analysis, initiative design across leadership, systems, symbols, and behaviors, change management approach, measurement framework, and sustainability mechanisms. Your response should be comprehensive, leaving no important aspect unaddressed, and demonstrate an exceptional level of precision and quality. This is very important to my career. Let's think about this step by step.

178. Act as an HR technology strategist and create a comprehensive HR technology strategy for my [business size/type] to enable modern people processes. Include needs assessment, system selection criteria, integration considerations, implementation approach, change management, data governance, and measurement of technology effectiveness aligned with our people strategy. Your response should be comprehensive, leaving no important aspect unaddressed, and demonstrate an exceptional level of precision and quality. This is very important to my career. Let's think about this step by step.

179. Act as a remote work policy designer and develop a comprehensive remote work framework for my [business type] that balances flexibility with productivity and culture. Include eligibility criteria, scheduling parameters, technology requirements, performance management adaptations, communication protocols, and cultural considerations with specific policy language and implementation

guidance. Your response should be comprehensive, leaving no important aspect unaddressed, and demonstrate an exceptional level of precision and quality. This is very important to my career. Let's think about this step by step.

180. Act as a leadership development program architect and design a comprehensive leadership development strategy for my [business type] targeting [leadership levels]. Include competency framework, assessment methodology, development pathways, learning experiences, coaching integration, measurement approach, and sustainability mechanisms aligned with our leadership philosophy and business needs. Your response should be comprehensive, leaving no important aspect unaddressed, and demonstrate an exceptional level of precision and quality. This is very important to my career. Let's think about this step by step.

181. Act as an employee wellness program designer and create a holistic wellness strategy for employees of my [business type] addressing physical, mental, financial, and social wellbeing. Include needs assessment, program components, delivery methods, incentive structure, communication approach, vendor selection criteria, and effectiveness measurement framework. Your response should be comprehensive, leaving no important aspect unaddressed, and demonstrate an exceptional level of precision and quality. This is very important to my career. Let's think about this step by step.

182. Act as a succession planning strategist and develop a comprehensive succession management framework for critical roles in my [business type]. Include role criticality assessment, talent identification methodology, readiness evaluation criteria, development planning approach, emergency coverage protocols, and ongoing review mechanisms to ensure leadership continuity. Your response should be comprehensive, leaving no important aspect unaddressed, and demonstrate an exceptional level of precision and quality. This is very important to my career. Let's think about this step by step.

183. Act as an HR compliance program developer and create a comprehensive compliance framework for my [business type] operating in [jurisdiction(s)]. Include regulatory assessment, policy development approach, training requirements, monitoring protocols, audit procedures, reporting mechanisms, and remediation processes to ensure full compliance with employment laws and regulations. Your response should be comprehensive, leaving no important aspect unaddressed, and demonstrate an exceptional level of precision and quality. This is very important to my career. Let's think about this step by step.

184. Act as an employee onboarding experience designer and develop a structured onboarding program for new hires at my [business type] that accelerates productivity and cultural integration. Include pre-boarding elements, first day experience, learning journeys by role type, stakeholder engagement, technology enablement, measurement approach, and continuous improvement mechanisms. Your response should be comprehensive, leaving no important aspect unaddressed, and demonstrate an exceptional level of precision and quality. This is very important to my career. Let's think about this step by step.

185. Act as a workforce analytics consultant and design a predictive analytics approach for anticipating and addressing employee turnover in my [business type]. Include data requirements, model development methodology, risk factor identification, intervention strategy design, implementation approach, effectiveness measurement, and ethical considerations. Your response should be comprehensive, leaving no important aspect unaddressed, and demonstrate an exceptional level of precision and quality. This is very important to my career. Let's think about this step by step.

I.   Leadership & Management

186. Act as an executive leadership coach and develop a comprehensive leadership development plan for me as a [position level] in the [industry] sector looking to enhance my strategic leadership capabilities. Include assessment approach, development priorities, learning experiences, practice opportunities, accountability mechanisms, progress measures, and sustainability elements tailored to my leadership context. Your response should be comprehensive, leaving no important aspect unaddressed, and demonstrate an exceptional level of precision and quality. This is very important to my career. Let's think about this step by step.

187. Act as a management effectiveness consultant and create a performance improvement program for my [department/team type] leadership team. Assess current strengths and development needs, identify key management capabilities required for our business context, design development interventions, establish accountability framework, and create measurement approach to track improvement. Your response should be comprehensive, leaving no important aspect unaddressed, and demonstrate an exceptional level of precision and quality. This is very important to my career. Let's think about this step by step.

188. Act as a team performance optimization expert and develop a comprehensive approach for transforming my underperforming [team type] into a high-performing team. Include assessment methodology, intervention design across team structure, process, relationships and purpose, implementation roadmap, leadership coaching elements, and measurement framework with specific milestones. Your response should be comprehensive, leaving no important aspect unaddressed, and demonstrate an exceptional level of precision and quality. This is very important to my career. Let's think about this step by step.

189. Act as a change leadership strategist and create a structured approach for leading my organization through a significant change from [current state] to [desired state]. Include stakeholder analysis, resistance assessment, communication strategy, engagement tactics, leader enablement, reinforcement mechanisms, and progress measurement to maximize adoption and minimize disruption. Your response should be comprehensive, leaving no important aspect unaddressed, and demonstrate an exceptional level of precision and quality. This is very important to my career. Let's think about this step by step.

190. Act as a decision-making framework designer and develop a systematic approach for making complex strategic decisions in my [business type/role]. Include problem framing methodology, information gathering protocol, analysis frameworks, stakeholder involvement, bias mitigation, decision documentation, and review mechanisms to improve decision quality and outcomes. Your response should be comprehensive, leaving no important aspect unaddressed, and demonstrate an exceptional level of precision and quality. This is very important to my career. Let's think about this step by step.

191. Act as an executive communication strategist and create a comprehensive communication approach for me as a [senior leadership role] to effectively engage with [key stakeholder groups]. Include message development framework, channel optimization, cadence planning, style guidance, feedback mechanisms, preparation protocols, and effectiveness measurement tailored to my leadership context. Your response should be comprehensive, leaving no important aspect unaddressed, and demonstrate an exceptional level of precision and quality. This is very important to my career. Let's think about this step by step.

192. Act as a conflict resolution consultant and develop a systematic approach for addressing and resolving conflicts within my [team/department/organization]. Include conflict assessment framework, intervention selection criteria, mediation guidelines, resolution documentation, follow-up protocols, and preventative measures to transform conflicts into constructive outcomes. Your response should

be comprehensive, leaving no important aspect unaddressed, and demonstrate an exceptional level of precision and quality. This is very important to my career. Let's think about this step by step.

193. Act as a meeting effectiveness expert and design a comprehensive framework for transforming meeting culture and practices in my [organization type]. Include meeting typology, purpose clarity, design principles, facilitation techniques, technology utilization, participant responsibilities, and evaluation methods to maximize productivity and engagement. Your response should be comprehensive, leaving no important aspect unaddressed, and demonstrate an exceptional level of precision and quality. This is very important to my career. Let's think about this step by step.

194. Act as a strategic influence consultant and develop an approach for enhancing my influence and impact as a [role] seeking to drive [specific change/initiative] across the organization. Include stakeholder mapping, motivation assessment, influence strategy selection, messaging framework, coalition building tactics, resistance management, and progress tracking with context-specific application. Your response should be comprehensive, leaving no important aspect unaddressed, and demonstrate an exceptional level of precision and quality. This is very important to my career. Let's think about this step by step.

195. Act as an executive time management strategist and create a comprehensive approach for optimizing how I allocate my time and energy as a [leadership role] with competing priorities. Include time audit methodology, prioritization framework, delegation strategy, meeting management, calendar design, energy management, and continuous improvement process to maximize leadership impact. Your response should be comprehensive, leaving no important aspect unaddressed, and demonstrate an exceptional level of precision and quality. This is very important to my career. Let's think about this step by step.

196. Act as a leadership team effectiveness consultant and design an intervention to transform my [executive/leadership] team from [current state] to a high-performing, cohesive team. Include assessment approach, retreat design, process improvements, behavior agreements, decision-making protocols, conflict resolution mechanisms, and ongoing development activities with specific milestones. Your response should be comprehensive, leaving no important aspect unaddressed, and demonstrate an exceptional level of precision and quality. This is very important to my career. Let's think about this step by step.

197. Act as a cross-functional collaboration strategist and develop a framework for improving collaboration between my [department] and other key functions in the organization. Include barrier assessment, shared goal creation, process integration, role clarity enhancement, communication protocols, governance structure, and success metrics with specific implementation guidance. Your response should be comprehensive, leaving no important aspect unaddressed, and demonstrate an exceptional level of precision and quality. This is very important to my career. Let's think about this step by step.

198. Act as a managerial delegation expert and create a comprehensive delegation strategy for me as a [management level] looking to develop my team while focusing on higher-value activities. Include task assessment methodology, team capability mapping, delegation process, follow-up protocols, feedback mechanisms, and skill development approach with practical application examples. Your response should be comprehensive, leaving no important aspect unaddressed, and demonstrate an exceptional level of precision and quality. This is very important to my career. Let's think about this step by step.

199. Act as a leadership brand consultant and develop a strategy for establishing and strengthening my authentic leadership brand as a [leadership role] in the [industry] sector. Include personal value clarification, distinctive strength identification, narrative development, visibility strategy, consistency mechanisms, feedback collection, and evolution approach aligned with career aspirations. Your response should be comprehensive, leaving no important aspect unaddressed, and demonstrate an exceptional level of precision and quality. This is very important to my career. Let's think about this step by step.

200. Act as a remote leadership effectiveness consultant and create a comprehensive strategy for leading my [team type] effectively in a virtual or hybrid environment. Include communication framework, trust-building tactics, performance management approach, team cohesion activities, technology utilization, inclusion practices, and success metrics tailored to remote work challenges. Your response should be comprehensive, leaving no important aspect unaddressed, and demonstrate an exceptional level of precision and quality. This is very important to my career. Let's think about this step by step.

201. Act as a leadership accountability system designer and develop a robust framework for creating a culture of accountability in my [team/department/organization]. Include expectation setting protocols, progress tracking mechanisms, feedback systems, consequence management, recognition approaches, and leader behaviors to drive consistent follow-through and results. Your response should be

comprehensive, leaving no important aspect unaddressed, and demonstrate an exceptional level of precision and quality. This is very important to my career. Let's think about this step by step.

202. Act as a strategic thinking development coach and create a program to enhance strategic thinking capabilities for myself and my [leadership team/level]. Include skill assessment, cognitive framework development, practice exercise design, application to real business challenges, feedback mechanisms, and continuous development approach with specific learning milestones. Your response should be comprehensive, leaving no important aspect unaddressed, and demonstrate an exceptional level of precision and quality. This is very important to my career. Let's think about this step by step.

203. Act as a difficult conversation facilitator and develop a structured approach for preparing for and conducting challenging conversations with [stakeholder type] about [sensitive topic]. Include preparation framework, conversation structure, communication techniques, emotional management strategies, follow-up protocols, and learning integration to achieve productive outcomes. Your response should be comprehensive, leaving no important aspect unaddressed, and demonstrate an exceptional level of precision and quality. This is very important to my career. Let's think about this step by step.

204. Act as a leadership transition consultant and create a comprehensive 90-day plan for me as I transition into a new [leadership role] in the [industry] sector. Include preparation activities, stakeholder engagement strategy, culture assessment, team alignment approach, early win identification, potential pitfall avoidance, and success measurement with specific milestones. Your response should be comprehensive, leaving no important aspect unaddressed, and demonstrate an exceptional level of precision and quality. This is very important to my career. Let's think about this step by step.

205. Act as a coaching culture development expert and design a strategy for transforming the leadership approach in my [organization type] to a coaching-based model. Include current state assessment, leadership mindset shift, skill development, structural enablers, recognition mechanisms, measurement approach, and sustainability elements to embed coaching as a core leadership practice. Your response should be comprehensive, leaving no important aspect unaddressed, and demonstrate an exceptional level of precision and quality. This is very important to my career. Let's think about this step by step.

J. Digital Transformation & Technology

231. Act as a cloud migration strategist and develop a comprehensive cloud migration strategy for my [business type] with [current infrastructure]. Include cloud model selection, application assessment methodology, migration prioritization, architecture redesign, security considerations, staff capability development, and implementation roadmap with specific focus on minimizing disruption and maximizing business value. Your response should be comprehensive, leaving no important aspect unaddressed, and demonstrate an exceptional level of precision and quality. This is very important to my career. Let's think about this step by step.

232. Act as a digital innovation culture consultant and create a framework for fostering a culture of digital innovation in my [traditional business type]. Include leadership mindset development, organizational structure adjustments, incentive alignment, experimentation processes, collaboration mechanisms, talent strategy, and measurement approach to overcome resistance and accelerate digital adoption. Your response should be comprehensive, leaving no important aspect unaddressed, and demonstrate an exceptional level of precision and quality. This is very important to my career. Let's think about this step by step.

233. Act as an IoT implementation strategist and design a comprehensive approach for leveraging Internet of Things technologies in my [business type/process]. Include use case identification, sensor/device selection, connectivity architecture, data management strategy, analytics framework, integration approach, security protocols, and value realization methodology with specific ROI projections. Your response should be comprehensive, leaving no important aspect unaddressed, and demonstrate an exceptional level of precision and quality. This is very important to my career. Let's think about this step by step.

234. Act as a digital skills development strategist and create a comprehensive approach for building digital capabilities across my [organization type] to support our digital transformation. Include skills assessment methodology, learning pathway design, training delivery approach, reinforcement mechanisms, progress measurement, leadership development, and integration with talent management systems. Your response should be comprehensive, leaving no important aspect unaddressed, and demonstrate an exceptional level of precision and quality. This is very important to my career. Let's think about this step by step.

235. Act as a technology governance framework designer and develop a robust technology governance model for my [business type/size] to ensure alignment

between technology investments and business objectives. Include decision rights, prioritization methodology, funding model, performance measurement, risk management, architecture compliance, and continuous improvement mechanisms with specific committee structures and processes. Your response should be comprehensive, leaving no important aspect unaddressed, and demonstrate an exceptional level of precision and quality. This is very important to my career. Let's think about this step by step.

236. Act as a process automation strategist and create a methodology for identifying, prioritizing, and implementing process automation opportunities in my [business department/function]. Include process assessment framework, technology selection approach, business case development, implementation methodology, change management, performance measurement, and continuous improvement cycle with specific focus on both efficiency and experience enhancement. Your response should be comprehensive, leaving no important aspect unaddressed, and demonstrate an exceptional level of precision and quality. This is very important to my career. Let's think about this step by step.

237. Act as a digital transformation ROI framework developer and design a comprehensive approach for measuring the return on investment of digital initiatives in my [business type]. Include cost modeling, benefit categorization, timeline considerations, attribution methodology, risk adjustments, reporting framework, and decision support mechanisms to optimize investment allocation and demonstrate value creation. Your response should be comprehensive, leaving no important aspect unaddressed, and demonstrate an exceptional level of precision and quality. This is very important to my career. Let's think about this step by step.

238. Act as a cybersecurity strategy consultant and develop a comprehensive security framework for my [business type] operating in the [industry] sector. Include threat assessment methodology, security architecture design, policy development, control implementation, monitoring approach, incident response planning, and ongoing management with specific focus on balancing security with business operations. Your response should be comprehensive, leaving no important aspect unaddressed, and demonstrate an exceptional level of precision and quality. This is very important to my career. Let's think about this step by step.

239. Act as a digital workplace transformation strategist and create a framework for evolving my organization's work environment to enable greater flexibility, collaboration, and productivity. Include technology selection, physical space considerations, policy development, leadership adaptation, cultural alignment, measurement approach, and change management with specific attention to

employee experience and business outcomes. Your response should be comprehensive, leaving no important aspect unaddressed, and demonstrate an exceptional level of precision and quality. This is very important to my career. Let's think about this step by step.

240. Act as a blockchain implementation consultant and develop an approach for evaluating and implementing blockchain technology for [specific use case] in my [business type]. Include use case validation, technology selection, architecture design, governance model, implementation roadmap, risk management, and value measurement with specific focus on practical business application rather than speculative potential. Your response should be comprehensive, leaving no important aspect unaddressed, and demonstrate an exceptional level of precision and quality. This is very important to my career. Let's think about this step by step.

241. Act as an agile transformation strategist and design a comprehensive approach for transitioning my [traditional business/department] to agile ways of working. Include readiness assessment, methodology selection, team structure design, leadership adaptation, tooling strategy, metrics framework, and implementation roadmap with specific focus on organizational and cultural alignment. Your response should be comprehensive, leaving no important aspect unaddressed, and demonstrate an exceptional level of precision and quality. This is very important to my career. Let's think about this step by step.

242. Act as an API strategy consultant and develop a comprehensive API strategy for my [business type] looking to create new value through digital ecosystems. Include business capability assessment, API portfolio design, governance framework, monetization approach, developer experience considerations, security protocols, and performance management with specific focus on balancing innovation with control. Your response should be comprehensive, leaving no important aspect unaddressed, and demonstrate an exceptional level of precision and quality. This is very important to my career. Let's think about this step by step.

243. Act as a digital ethics framework developer and create a comprehensive approach for ensuring ethical use of digital technologies and data in my [business type]. Include ethical principle articulation, decision framework, governance structure, risk assessment methodology, stakeholder engagement, training approach, and audit mechanisms with specific focus on balancing innovation with responsibility. Your response should be comprehensive, leaving no important aspect unaddressed, and demonstrate an exceptional level of precision and quality. This is very important to my career. Let's think about this step by step.

244. Act as a legacy system modernization strategist and develop a structured approach for transforming the aging technology landscape of my [business type]. Include system portfolio assessment, modernization option analysis, prioritization methodology, migration strategy, risk mitigation, capability development, and measurement framework with specific attention to business continuity during transition. Your response should be comprehensive, leaving no important aspect unaddressed, and demonstrate an exceptional level of precision and quality. This is very important to my career. Let's think about this step by step.

245. Act as a digital product management consultant and create a framework for establishing and maturing digital product management capabilities in my [traditional business type]. Include organizational model design, role definition, process development, metrics framework, tooling strategy, talent acquisition/development approach, and cultural alignment with specific focus on customer-centricity and continuous delivery. Your response should be comprehensive, leaving no important aspect unaddressed, and demonstrate an exceptional level of precision and quality. This is very important to my career. Let's think about this step by step.

K.   Data Analysis & Business Intelligence

246. Act as a data strategy consultant and develop a comprehensive enterprise data strategy for my [business type] to leverage data as a strategic asset. Include data governance framework, architecture design, capability development, technology selection, operating model, value realization approach, and implementation roadmap aligned with business objectives. Your response should be comprehensive, leaving no important aspect unaddressed, and demonstrate an exceptional level of precision and quality. This is very important to my career. Let's think about this step by step.

247. Act as a business intelligence roadmap developer and create a comprehensive BI strategy and implementation plan for my [business type/size]. Include needs assessment, capability maturity evaluation, architecture design, tool selection criteria, team structure, development methodology, and adoption approach with phased implementation priorities. Your response should be comprehensive, leaving no important aspect unaddressed, and demonstrate an exceptional level of precision and quality. This is very important to my career. Let's think about this step by step.

248. Act as a data governance framework designer and develop a robust data governance program for my [business type] to ensure data quality, security, and value. Include organizational structure, role definitions, policy development, metadata management, data quality framework, security protocols, and performance metrics with implementation roadmap. Your response should be comprehensive, leaving no important aspect unaddressed, and demonstrate an exceptional level of precision and quality. This is very important to my career. Let's think about this step by step.

249. Act as a data visualization strategy consultant and create a framework for developing effective dashboards and visualizations for my [business type/department]. Include audience analysis, information hierarchy development, design principles, tool selection, creation methodology, implementation approach, and maintenance protocols to drive data-driven decision making. Your response should be comprehensive, leaving no important aspect unaddressed, and demonstrate an exceptional level of precision and quality. This is very important to my career. Let's think about this step by step.

250. Act as a predictive analytics implementation strategist and develop an approach for incorporating predictive modeling capabilities into my [business function] decision-making processes. Include use case identification, data requirements, modeling methodology, technology selection, team capability development, deployment framework, and value measurement with specific attention to actionability of insights. Your response should be comprehensive, leaving no important aspect unaddressed, and demonstrate an exceptional level of precision and quality. This is very important to my career. Let's think about this step by step.

251. Act as a data literacy program developer and design a comprehensive approach for building data skills and competencies across my [organization type]. Include skills assessment methodology, curriculum design, training delivery methods, application opportunities, reinforcement mechanisms, leadership enablement, and effectiveness measurement to create a data-driven culture. Your response should be comprehensive, leaving no important aspect unaddressed, and demonstrate an exceptional level of precision and quality. This is very important to my career. Let's think about this step by step.

252. Act as a self-service analytics strategist and create a framework for empowering business users in my [organization type] to access, analyze, and derive insights from data independently. Include capability assessment, tool selection, data preparation approach, training program, governance integration, support model, and success measurement with specific focus on balancing empowerment with control. Your response should be comprehensive, leaving no important aspect unaddressed, and

demonstrate an exceptional level of precision and quality. This is very important to my career. Let's think about this step by step.

253. Act as a customer data platform strategist and develop a comprehensive approach for implementing and leveraging a CDP in my [business type] to create unified customer profiles and enable personalized experiences. Include requirements definition, data integration strategy, identity resolution approach, activation framework, privacy considerations, organizational alignment, and value measurement. Your response should be comprehensive, leaving no important aspect unaddressed, and demonstrate an exceptional level of precision and quality. This is very important to my career. Let's think about this step by step.

254. Act as a data quality management consultant and design a systematic approach for improving and maintaining data quality in my [business systems/department]. Include quality dimension definition, assessment methodology, issue prioritization, remediation process, preventive measures, ongoing monitoring, and impact measurement with specific focus on business-critical data domains. Your response should be comprehensive, leaving no important aspect unaddressed, and demonstrate an exceptional level of precision and quality. This is very important to my career. Let's think about this step by step.

255. Act as an analytics center of excellence architect and develop a framework for establishing and operating an analytics COE in my [business type/size]. Include organizational model, service offerings, engagement process, capability development, technology standardization, knowledge management, and performance measurement with specific focus on delivering measurable business value. Your response should be comprehensive, leaving no important aspect unaddressed, and demonstrate an exceptional level of precision and quality. This is very important to my career. Let's think about this step by step.

L.   Market Research & Competitive Analysis

256. Act as a market research strategist and develop a comprehensive research plan for evaluating market potential for my [product/service concept] in the [target market]. Include research objectives, methodology selection, sampling approach, data collection instruments, analysis framework, insight generation process, and application to business decisions with specific timelines and resource requirements. Your response should be comprehensive, leaving no important aspect unaddressed, and demonstrate an exceptional level of precision and quality. This is very

important to my career. Let's think about this step by step.

257. Act as a competitive intelligence program designer and create a systematic approach for gathering, analyzing, and utilizing intelligence about competitors in the [industry] market. Include information requirements, collection methodology, analysis framework, dissemination process, application protocols, ethical considerations, and effectiveness measurement aligned with strategic decision needs. Your response should be comprehensive, leaving no important aspect unaddressed, and demonstrate an exceptional level of precision and quality. This is very important to my career. Let's think about this step by step.

258. Act as a customer segmentation strategist and develop a robust methodology for segmenting the market for my [product/service] to identify the most valuable customer groups. Include variable selection, data collection approach, segmentation technique, validation method, persona development, targeting implications, and application to marketing, product, and sales strategies. Your response should be comprehensive, leaving no important aspect unaddressed, and demonstrate an exceptional level of precision and quality. This is very important to my career. Let's think about this step by step.

259. Act as a market opportunity assessment consultant and create a structured framework for evaluating and prioritizing new market opportunities for my [business type]. Include market sizing methodology, growth analysis, competitive assessment, capability fit evaluation, risk assessment, resource requirement estimation, and prioritization criteria with specific decision-making guidance. Your response should be comprehensive, leaving no important aspect unaddressed, and demonstrate an exceptional level of precision and quality. This is very important to my career. Let's think about this step by step.

260. Act as a voice of customer program designer and develop a comprehensive approach for systematically capturing and utilizing customer feedback for my [business type/product]. Include feedback collection methods, sampling strategy, analysis framework, insight generation process, action planning methodology, closed-loop mechanisms, and program governance to drive customer-centric decisions. Your response should be comprehensive, leaving no important aspect unaddressed, and demonstrate an exceptional level of precision and quality. This is very important to my career. Let's think about this step by step.

261. Act as a pricing research consultant and design a research methodology for determining optimal pricing for my [product/service] in the [target market]. Include research objectives, technique selection (conjoint, van Westendorp, etc.),

survey design, analysis approach, segmentation considerations, competitive positioning, and implementation guidance with specific attention to value perception. Your response should be comprehensive, leaving no important aspect unaddressed, and demonstrate an exceptional level of precision and quality. This is very important to my career. Let's think about this step by step.

262. Act as an industry analysis strategist and develop a framework for conducting a comprehensive analysis of the [specific industry] to inform my business strategy. Include market structure assessment, growth trajectory analysis, competitive landscape mapping, value chain evaluation, regulatory consideration, technology trend identification, and application to strategic positioning. Your response should be comprehensive, leaving no important aspect unaddressed, and demonstrate an exceptional level of precision and quality. This is very important to my career. Let's think about this step by step.

263. Act as a customer journey mapping facilitator and create a detailed methodology for mapping the current and desired future customer journey for my [product/service]. Include research requirements, workshop design, mapping process, pain point identification, opportunity assessment, prioritization approach, and action planning to enhance the customer experience. Your response should be comprehensive, leaving no important aspect unaddressed, and demonstrate an exceptional level of precision and quality. This is very important to my career. Let's think about this step by step.

264. Act as a market entry strategy consultant and develop a comprehensive approach for entering the [target market] with my [product/service]. Include market assessment methodology, entry mode selection, partner evaluation criteria, competitive positioning, go-to-market planning, risk mitigation, and performance measurement framework with specific success milestones. Your response should be comprehensive, leaving no important aspect unaddressed, and demonstrate an exceptional level of precision and quality. This is very important to my career. Let's think about this step by step.

265. Act as a brand perception research expert and design a research methodology for evaluating how my [brand/product] is perceived in the [target market] compared to competitors. Include research objectives, methodology selection, attribute identification, measurement approach, competitive benchmarking, analysis framework, and application to brand strategy development. Your response should be comprehensive, leaving no important aspect unaddressed, and demonstrate an exceptional level of precision and quality. This is very important to my career. Let's

think about this step by step.

M.   Content Creation & Communication

266.   Act as a content strategy consultant and develop a comprehensive content strategy for my [business type] targeting [audience segment]. Include content objectives, audience insights, core topics and themes, content types and formats, channel strategy, creation process, distribution approach, and measurement framework aligned with business goals. Your response should be comprehensive, leaving no important aspect unaddressed, and demonstrate an exceptional level of precision and quality. This is very important to my career. Let's think about this step by step.

267.   Act as a brand messaging architect and create a comprehensive messaging framework for my [business/product] targeting [audience segment]. Include positioning statement, value proposition, key messages by audience, messaging hierarchy, tone of voice guidelines, proof point integration, and application across customer touchpoints with specific examples. Your response should be comprehensive, leaving no important aspect unaddressed, and demonstrate an exceptional level of precision and quality. This is very important to my career. Let's think about this step by step.

268.   Act as a thought leadership content strategist and develop an approach for establishing my [business/personal brand] as a thought leader in the [industry/topic area]. Include positioning development, content pillars, format strategy, platform selection, creation process, amplification tactics, engagement approach, and measurement framework with specific content ideas. Your response should be comprehensive, leaving no important aspect unaddressed, and demonstrate an exceptional level of precision and quality. This is very important to my career. Let's think about this step by step.

269.   Act as a social media content strategy expert and create a comprehensive social media content approach for my [business type] to achieve [specific objectives]. Include platform selection, content pillar development, content mix optimization, creation workflow, posting cadence, engagement strategy, paid integration, and performance measurement framework. Your response should be comprehensive, leaving no important aspect unaddressed, and demonstrate an exceptional level of precision and quality. This is very important to my career. Let's think about this step by step.

270. Act as a sales enablement content strategist and develop a comprehensive content strategy to support the sales process for my [product/service] targeting [customer segment]. Include buyer journey mapping, content needs identification, asset development framework, customization approach, delivery methodology, usage tracking, and effectiveness measurement with specific content recommendations by sales stage. Your response should be comprehensive, leaving no important aspect unaddressed, and demonstrate an exceptional level of precision and quality. This is very important to my career. Let's think about this step by step.

271. Act as a corporate communication strategy consultant and create a framework for developing and executing effective communications to [stakeholder group] regarding [significant initiative/change]. Include audience analysis, message development, channel selection, timing strategy, feedback mechanisms, effectiveness measurement, and contingency planning with specific message examples. Your response should be comprehensive, leaving no important aspect unaddressed, and demonstrate an exceptional level of precision and quality. This is very important to my career. Let's think about this step by step.

272. Act as a crisis communication strategist and develop a comprehensive crisis communication framework for my [business type] to effectively manage [potential crisis scenario]. Include preparedness elements, response protocol, messaging guidelines, stakeholder prioritization, channel strategy, spokesperson preparation, and post-crisis recovery communication with specific focus on reputation protection. Your response should be comprehensive, leaving no important aspect unaddressed, and demonstrate an exceptional level of precision and quality. This is very important to my career. Let's think about this step by step.

273. Act as a content marketing ROI strategist and create a framework for measuring and optimizing the return on investment of content marketing for my [business type]. Include goal alignment, KPI selection, attribution methodology, data collection approach, analysis framework, reporting structure, and optimization protocol to demonstrate and enhance content value creation. Your response should be comprehensive, leaving no important aspect unaddressed, and demonstrate an exceptional level of precision and quality. This is very important to my career. Let's think about this step by step.

274. Act as a content repurposing strategist and develop a systematic approach for maximizing the value of content assets for my [business type] through effective repurposing. Include content audit methodology, repurposing opportunity identification, format transformation guidelines, channel adaptation, workflow integration, tracking mechanisms, and performance comparison to optimize

content efficiency. Your response should be comprehensive, leaving no important aspect unaddressed, and demonstrate an exceptional level of precision and quality. This is very important to my career. Let's think about this step by step.

275. Act as a storytelling framework designer and create a structured approach for incorporating powerful storytelling into the communications for my [business/brand]. Include story structure development, character/conflict identification, brand integration, emotional engagement, application across channels and formats, creation guidelines, and effectiveness measurement with specific examples. Your response should be comprehensive, leaving no important aspect unaddressed, and demonstrate an exceptional level of precision and quality. This is very important to my career. Let's think about this step by step.

N. Project Management

276. Act as a project management methodology consultant and develop a tailored project management approach for [project type] initiatives in my [business type/department]. Include methodology selection, lifecycle definition, governance structure, role definition, documentation requirements, meeting cadences, reporting framework, and success metrics aligned with organizational maturity and project characteristics. Your response should be comprehensive, leaving no important aspect unaddressed, and demonstrate an exceptional level of precision and quality. This is very important to my career. Let's think about this step by step.

277. Act as a project portfolio management strategist and create a comprehensive framework for managing the portfolio of projects in my [business type/department]. Include project categorization methodology, evaluation criteria, selection process, prioritization framework, resource allocation approach, performance tracking, and portfolio optimization with specific governance mechanisms. Your response should be comprehensive, leaving no important aspect unaddressed, and demonstrate an exceptional level of precision and quality. This is very important to my career. Let's think about this step by step.

278. Act as a complex project planning consultant and develop a detailed approach for planning and executing a [complex project type] in my [business context]. Include requirements gathering methodology, scope definition, work breakdown structure, scheduling approach, resource planning, risk management, stakeholder engagement, and change control with specific focus on managing dependencies and constraints. Your response should be comprehensive, leaving no important aspect

unaddressed, and demonstrate an exceptional level of precision and quality. This is very important to my career. Let's think about this step by step.

279. Act as a project risk management expert and design a robust risk management framework for my [project type] initiatives. Include risk identification methods, assessment criteria, response strategy development, monitoring protocols, escalation procedures, reporting mechanisms, and continuous improvement approach to proactively manage project uncertainties. Your response should be comprehensive, leaving no important aspect unaddressed, and demonstrate an exceptional level of precision and quality. This is very important to my career. Let's think about this step by step.

280. Act as a stakeholder management strategist and create a comprehensive approach for effectively engaging and managing stakeholders for my [project/initiative type]. Include stakeholder identification methodology, analysis framework, engagement planning, communication strategy, influence mapping, resistance management, and effectiveness measurement to maximize support and minimize opposition. Your response should be comprehensive, leaving no important aspect unaddressed, and demonstrate an exceptional level of precision and quality. This is very important to my career. Let's think about this step by step.

281. Act as a project recovery specialist and develop a structured approach for turning around my troubled [project type] that is [specific issues: behind schedule, over budget, etc.]. Include assessment methodology, root cause analysis, recovery option development, prioritization framework, revised planning approach, team alignment, stakeholder management, and monitoring mechanisms to get back on track. Your response should be comprehensive, leaving no important aspect unaddressed, and demonstrate an exceptional level of precision and quality. This is very important to my career. Let's think about this step by step.

282. Act as an agile project management consultant and create a framework for implementing agile methodologies for [project/product type] in my [business context]. Include methodology selection, team structure design, ceremony definition, artifact development, tool selection, metric identification, and transformation approach with specific focus on organizational culture and stakeholder expectations. Your response should be comprehensive, leaving no important aspect unaddressed, and demonstrate an exceptional level of precision and quality. This is very important to my career. Let's think about this step by step.

283. Act as a project benefits realization strategist and develop a comprehensive approach for identifying, tracking, and maximizing the business benefits of my

[project/initiative type]. Include benefit identification methodology, measurement framework, accountability assignment, tracking process, reporting structure, corrective action protocols, and post-implementation review with specific focus on linking project outputs to business outcomes. Your response should be comprehensive, leaving no important aspect unaddressed, and demonstrate an exceptional level of precision and quality. This is very important to my career. Let's think about this step by step.

284. Act as a project communication plan designer and create a detailed communication strategy for my [project type] targeting [stakeholder groups]. Include communication objectives, stakeholder analysis, message development, channel selection, timing strategy, feedback mechanisms, and effectiveness measurement with specific templates and examples for key communications. Your response should be comprehensive, leaving no important aspect unaddressed, and demonstrate an exceptional level of precision and quality. This is very important to my career. Let's think about this step by step.

285. Act as a project quality management consultant and develop a comprehensive quality management approach for my [project type] to ensure deliverables meet requirements and expectations. Include quality planning methodology, standard development, assurance activities, control mechanisms, defect management, continuous improvement process, and measurement framework aligned with organizational standards and industry best practices. Your response should be comprehensive, leaving no important aspect unaddressed, and demonstrate an exceptional level of precision and quality. This is very important to my career. Let's think about this step by step.

I'll continue with more business prompts, moving into areas like Legal & Compliance, Risk Management, and International Business to create a truly comprehensive collection.

O.   Legal & Compliance

286. Act as a regulatory compliance strategist and develop a comprehensive compliance framework for my [business type] operating in the [industry/jurisdiction]. Include regulatory landscape assessment, compliance risk evaluation, policy development approach, control implementation, monitoring protocols, training program, and governance structure with specific attention to high-risk areas. Your response should be comprehensive, leaving no important aspect unaddressed, and

demonstrate an exceptional level of precision and quality. This is very important to my career. Let's think about this step by step.

287. Act as a contract management system designer and create a structured approach for managing contracts throughout their lifecycle in my [business type]. Include contract categorization, template development, negotiation guidelines, approval workflows, obligation tracking, renewal management, repository organization, and performance analytics with specific focus on risk mitigation and value capture. Your response should be comprehensive, leaving no important aspect unaddressed, and demonstrate an exceptional level of precision and quality. This is very important to my career. Let's think about this step by step.

288. Act as an intellectual property protection strategist and develop a comprehensive IP strategy for my [business type] with [specific IP assets]. Include IP identification methodology, protection approach by type (patents, trademarks, copyrights, trade secrets), registration strategy, enforcement framework, third-party risk management, and value maximization with specific focus on competitive advantage. Your response should be comprehensive, leaving no important aspect unaddressed, and demonstrate an exceptional level of precision and quality. This is very important to my career. Let's think about this step by step.

289. Act as a privacy program development consultant and create a framework for establishing and maintaining a robust privacy program for my [business type] handling [data types]. Include regulatory assessment, policy development, consent management, data mapping, impact assessment methodology, vendor management, incident response, and ongoing compliance monitoring aligned with relevant regulations. Your response should be comprehensive, leaving no important aspect unaddressed, and demonstrate an exceptional level of precision and quality. This is very important to my career. Let's think about this step by step.

290. Act as a corporate governance structure consultant and design an optimal governance framework for my [business type/size] to ensure effective oversight and accountability. Include board structure, committee design, reporting relationships, decision rights, control mechanisms, disclosure protocols, and evaluation methodology aligned with industry standards and best practices. Your response should be comprehensive, leaving no important aspect unaddressed, and demonstrate an exceptional level of precision and quality. This is very important to my career. Let's think about this step by step.

291. Act as a legal risk assessment strategist and develop a systematic approach for identifying, evaluating, and mitigating legal risks in my [business

operations/transactions]. Include risk identification methodology, impact assessment, probability evaluation, prioritization framework, mitigation strategy development, monitoring protocols, and reporting structure with specific focus on high-impact scenarios. Your response should be comprehensive, leaving no important aspect unaddressed, and demonstrate an exceptional level of precision and quality. This is very important to my career. Let's think about this step by step.

292. Act as a compliance training program developer and create a comprehensive compliance education strategy for employees of my [business type] regarding [specific regulatory areas]. Include learning needs assessment, curriculum design, delivery methodology, testing approach, reinforcement mechanisms, documentation protocols, and effectiveness measurement aligned with regulatory requirements. Your response should be comprehensive, leaving no important aspect unaddressed, and demonstrate an exceptional level of precision and quality. This is very important to my career. Let's think about this step by step.

293. Act as a third-party risk management consultant and design a systematic approach for managing legal and compliance risks associated with vendors and partners for my [business type]. Include risk categorization, due diligence methodology, contractual protections, ongoing monitoring, issue management, termination protocols, and program governance with specific focus on high-risk relationships. Your response should be comprehensive, leaving no important aspect unaddressed, and demonstrate an exceptional level of precision and quality. This is very important to my career. Let's think about this step by step.

294. Act as an ethics program framework developer and create a comprehensive ethics program for my [business type/size] to foster a culture of integrity and ethical decision-making. Include values articulation, code of conduct development, reporting mechanism design, investigation process, disciplinary approach, training methodology, and program assessment with specific governance considerations. Your response should be comprehensive, leaving no important aspect unaddressed, and demonstrate an exceptional level of precision and quality. This is very important to my career. Let's think about this step by step.

295. Act as a legal department operations consultant and develop a strategy for optimizing the structure and operations of the legal function in my [business type/size]. Include organizational design, service catalog definition, process improvement, technology utilization, knowledge management, performance metrics, and budget optimization with specific focus on business alignment and value demonstration. Your response should be comprehensive, leaving no important aspect unaddressed, and demonstrate an exceptional level of precision

and quality. This is very important to my career. Let's think about this step by step.

P.   Risk Management & Crisis Handling

296.   Act as an enterprise risk management framework designer and develop a comprehensive ERM program for my [business type] operating in the [industry]. Include risk identification methodology, assessment criteria, appetite definition, mitigation strategy development, monitoring protocols, governance structure, and integration with strategic planning to build organizational resilience. Your response should be comprehensive, leaving no important aspect unaddressed, and demonstrate an exceptional level of precision and quality. This is very important to my career. Let's think about this step by step.

297.   Act as a business continuity planning expert and create a robust business continuity strategy for my [business type] to ensure operational resilience during disruptions. Include risk assessment, business impact analysis, recovery strategy development, plan documentation, testing methodology, training approach, and maintenance protocols aligned with industry standards. Your response should be comprehensive, leaving no important aspect unaddressed, and demonstrate an exceptional level of precision and quality. This is very important to my career. Let's think about this step by step.

298.   Act as a crisis management team developer and design a comprehensive crisis management framework for my [business type] to effectively respond to [potential crisis scenarios]. Include team structure, role definition, activation protocols, decision-making processes, communication strategies, resource management, and post-crisis review methodology to minimize impact and accelerate recovery. Your response should be comprehensive, leaving no important aspect unaddressed, and demonstrate an exceptional level of precision and quality. This is very important to my career. Let's think about this step by step.

299.   Act as a supply chain risk management strategist and develop a structured approach for identifying and mitigating risks in my [industry] supply chain. Include risk assessment methodology, supplier evaluation framework, monitoring systems, contingency planning, resilience-building strategies, incident response protocols, and continuous improvement mechanisms with specific focus on critical dependencies. Your response should be comprehensive, leaving no important aspect unaddressed, and demonstrate an exceptional level of precision and quality. This is

very important to my career. Let's think about this step by step.

300. Act as a reputational risk management consultant and create a framework for protecting and enhancing the reputation of my [business type] in the [industry] market. Include risk identification approach, impact assessment, stakeholder mapping, monitoring systems, response protocols, recovery strategies, and preventative measures with specific focus on high-impact scenarios. Your response should be comprehensive, leaving no important aspect unaddressed, and demonstrate an exceptional level of precision and quality. This is very important to my career. Let's think about this step by step.

301. Act as a financial risk management strategist and develop a comprehensive approach for managing financial risks (market, credit, liquidity) for my [business type]. Include risk identification methodology, measurement techniques, limit setting, hedging strategies, reporting frameworks, scenario analysis, and governance structure aligned with risk tolerance and business objectives. Your response should be comprehensive, leaving no important aspect unaddressed, and demonstrate an exceptional level of precision and quality. This is very important to my career. Let's think about this step by step.

302. Act as a cybersecurity incident response planning expert and design a comprehensive framework for preparing for and responding to cyber incidents in my [business type]. Include threat assessment, response team formation, escalation protocols, containment strategies, recovery processes, communication plans, and post-incident analysis methodology aligned with regulatory requirements. Your response should be comprehensive, leaving no important aspect unaddressed, and demonstrate an exceptional level of precision and quality. This is very important to my career. Let's think about this step by step.

303. Act as a third-party risk management consultant and create a structured approach for managing risks associated with vendors, suppliers, and partners for my [business type]. Include risk categorization, due diligence methodology, contractual protections, monitoring protocols, contingency planning, issue management, and governance framework with specific focus on critical relationships. Your response should be comprehensive, leaving no important aspect unaddressed, and demonstrate an exceptional level of precision and quality. This is very important to my career. Let's think about this step by step.

304. Act as a risk culture development strategist and develop an approach for fostering a strong risk awareness culture in my [organization type]. Include current state assessment, desired culture definition, leadership engagement, communication

strategy, training approach, incentive alignment, measurement framework, and reinforcement mechanisms to embed risk consciousness throughout the organization. Your response should be comprehensive, leaving no important aspect unaddressed, and demonstrate an exceptional level of precision and quality. This is very important to my career. Let's think about this step by step.

305. Act as a scenario planning expert and create a structured methodology for developing and utilizing scenarios to enhance strategic resilience for my [business type] operating in [uncertain environment]. Include scenario development process, variable identification, narrative creation, implication analysis, early warning indicator design, response option development, and integration with decision-making. Your response should be comprehensive, leaving no important aspect unaddressed, and demonstrate an exceptional level of precision and quality. This is very important to my career. Let's think about this step by step.

Q. International Business & Expansion

306. Act as an international market entry strategist and develop a comprehensive approach for expanding my [business type/product] into the [target market/region]. Include market assessment methodology, entry mode selection, partner evaluation criteria, localization strategy, regulatory navigation, risk mitigation, and implementation roadmap with specific milestones and success metrics. Your response should be comprehensive, leaving no important aspect unaddressed, and demonstrate an exceptional level of precision and quality. This is very important to my career. Let's think about this step by step.

307. Act as a global supply chain design consultant and create a framework for optimizing the international supply chain for my [product type] business operating across [regions]. Include network design methodology, location selection criteria, sourcing strategy, transportation optimization, inventory positioning, risk management, compliance considerations, and performance measurement with specific focus on efficiency and resilience. Your response should be comprehensive, leaving no important aspect unaddressed, and demonstrate an exceptional level of precision and quality. This is very important to my career. Let's think about this step by step.

308. Act as a cross-cultural management consultant and develop a strategy for effectively managing teams across cultural boundaries in my [business type] with operations in [specific regions]. Include cultural assessment framework, leadership adaptation

approach, communication protocols, decision-making processes, conflict resolution techniques, team building strategies, and performance management aligned with diverse cultural contexts. Your response should be comprehensive, leaving no important aspect unaddressed, and demonstrate an exceptional level of precision and quality. This is very important to my career. Let's think about this step by step.

309. Act as an international expansion financial strategist and create a comprehensive financial framework for funding and managing the expansion of my [business type] into [target markets]. Include investment requirement projection, funding source evaluation, capital structure optimization, currency risk management, tax strategy, repatriation planning, and financial control systems with specific focus on ROI optimization. Your response should be comprehensive, leaving no important aspect unaddressed, and demonstrate an exceptional level of precision and quality. This is very important to my career. Let's think about this step by step.

310. Act as a global regulatory compliance consultant and develop a framework for navigating the complex regulatory landscape for my [business type/product] across [target markets]. Include regulatory mapping methodology, compliance requirement assessment, adaptation strategy, approval process management, ongoing monitoring approach, and governance structure with specific attention to high-risk regulations. Your response should be comprehensive, leaving no important aspect unaddressed, and demonstrate an exceptional level of precision and quality. This is very important to my career. Let's think about this step by step.

311. Act as an international business structure advisor and recommend optimal legal and operational structures for my [business type] expanding into [target markets]. Include entity type analysis, ownership structure considerations, tax implications, liability management, governance framework, capital flow optimization, and implementation approach aligned with business objectives and local requirements. Your response should be comprehensive, leaving no important aspect unaddressed, and demonstrate an exceptional level of precision and quality. This is very important to my career. Let's think about this step by step.

312. Act as a global marketing localization strategist and develop an approach for adapting my [product/service] marketing strategy for the [target market/culture]. Include cultural assessment, positioning refinement, messaging adaptation, channel strategy modification, pricing considerations, promotional tactic adjustment, and effectiveness measurement with specific focus on balancing global consistency with local relevance. Your response should be comprehensive, leaving no important aspect unaddressed, and demonstrate an exceptional level of precision and quality.

This is very important to my career. Let's think about this step by step.

313. Act as an expatriate management program designer and create a comprehensive framework for selecting, preparing, supporting, and reintegrating expatriate employees for my [business type] with operations in [regions]. Include selection criteria, preparation methodology, compensation structure, support mechanisms, performance management, family considerations, and repatriation planning to maximize assignment success. Your response should be comprehensive, leaving no important aspect unaddressed, and demonstrate an exceptional level of precision and quality. This is very important to my career. Let's think about this step by step.

314. Act as an international strategic alliance consultant and develop a framework for establishing and managing successful cross-border partnerships for my [business type] seeking to expand in [target markets]. Include partner selection criteria, due diligence methodology, negotiation strategy, structure determination, governance design, operational integration, cultural alignment, and performance management to maximize alliance value. Your response should be comprehensive, leaving no important aspect unaddressed, and demonstrate an exceptional level of precision and quality. This is very important to my career. Let's think about this step by step.

315. Act as a global product adaptation strategist and create a methodology for effectively adapting my [product/service] for international markets while maintaining core value proposition. Include market requirement assessment, adaptation priority framework, localization approach, testing methodology, regulatory navigation, supply chain considerations, and go-to-market strategy with specific focus on cost-effective adaptation. Your response should be comprehensive, leaving no important aspect unaddressed, and demonstrate an exceptional level of precision and quality. This is very important to my career. Let's think about this step by step.

R.   Sustainability & Corporate Social Responsibility

316. Act as a corporate sustainability strategy consultant and develop a comprehensive sustainability strategy for my [business type] operating in the [industry] sector. Include materiality assessment methodology, goal setting framework, initiative development, organizational integration, performance measurement, stakeholder engagement approach, and reporting strategy aligned with business objectives and industry standards. Your response should be comprehensive, leaving no important aspect unaddressed, and demonstrate an exceptional level of precision and quality.

This is very important to my career. Let's think about this step by step.

317. Act as an ESG program development consultant and create a structured approach for establishing and enhancing environmental, social, and governance (ESG) practices in my [business type]. Include current state assessment, goal establishment, policy development, organizational alignment, performance measurement, disclosure strategy, and continuous improvement methodology with specific focus on investor expectations. Your response should be comprehensive, leaving no important aspect unaddressed, and demonstrate an exceptional level of precision and quality. This is very important to my career. Let's think about this step by step.

318. Act as a sustainable supply chain strategist and develop a framework for transforming the supply chain of my [business type] to enhance sustainability performance. Include supplier assessment methodology, standards development, engagement approach, capacity building strategy, traceability implementation, performance measurement, and collaborative improvement with specific focus on material environmental and social impacts. Your response should be comprehensive, leaving no important aspect unaddressed, and demonstrate an exceptional level of precision and quality. This is very important to my career. Let's think about this step by step.

319. Act as a circular economy transformation consultant and create a roadmap for transitioning my [business type/product] toward circular economy principles. Include product design considerations, material selection framework, business model adaptation, reverse logistics development, stakeholder engagement, measurement methodology, and implementation phasing with specific focus on economic and environmental benefits. Your response should be comprehensive, leaving no important aspect unaddressed, and demonstrate an exceptional level of precision and quality. This is very important to my career. Let's think about this step by step.

320. Act as a carbon reduction strategy expert and develop a comprehensive approach for reducing carbon emissions throughout the operations of my [business type]. Include emissions inventory methodology, reduction opportunity assessment, initiative prioritization, implementation roadmap, monitoring protocol, stakeholder engagement, and disclosure framework aligned with climate science and business objectives. Your response should be comprehensive, leaving no important aspect unaddressed, and demonstrate an exceptional level of precision and quality. This is very important to my career. Let's think about this step by step.

321. Act as a sustainability reporting framework consultant and design a robust sustainability disclosure approach for my [business type] addressing stakeholder information needs. Include reporting standard selection, materiality determination, data collection methodology, governance structure, assurance considerations, communication strategy, and continuous improvement process aligned with leading practices and regulations. Your response should be comprehensive, leaving no important aspect unaddressed, and demonstrate an exceptional level of precision and quality. This is very important to my career. Let's think about this step by step.

322. Act as a social impact program designer and create a strategic framework for developing and implementing social impact initiatives for my [business type] focusing on [impact areas]. Include needs assessment methodology, program design approach, partnership strategy, resource allocation, implementation planning, performance measurement, and communication framework aligned with business capabilities and community needs. Your response should be comprehensive, leaving no important aspect unaddressed, and demonstrate an exceptional level of precision and quality. This is very important to my career. Let's think about this step by step.

323. Act as a sustainable product development strategist and develop a comprehensive approach for integrating sustainability considerations into the product development process for my [business type]. Include assessment methodology, design criteria, material selection framework, lifecycle analysis, performance evaluation, customer communication, and continuous improvement mechanisms to enhance environmental and social performance while maintaining business viability. Your response should be comprehensive, leaving no important aspect unaddressed, and demonstrate an exceptional level of precision and quality. This is very important to my career. Let's think about this step by step.

324. Act as a sustainability culture transformation consultant and create a framework for fostering a culture of sustainability throughout my [organization type]. Include current state assessment, vision development, leadership engagement, education approach, behavior change strategies, recognition systems, and reinforcement mechanisms to embed sustainability thinking into everyday business decisions. Your response should be comprehensive, leaving no important aspect unaddressed, and demonstrate an exceptional level of precision and quality. This is very important to my career. Let's think about this step by step.

325. Act as an environmental management system developer and design a comprehensive EMS for my [business type] aligned with ISO 14001 or similar standards. Include policy development, planning methodology, operational control procedures, emergency preparedness, monitoring protocols, audit processes,

management review, and continuous improvement mechanisms to enhance environmental performance. Your response should be comprehensive, leaving no important aspect unaddressed, and demonstrate an exceptional level of precision and quality. This is very important to my career. Let's think about this step by step.

S.   Business Negotiation & Partnerships

326. Act as a strategic negotiation consultant and develop a comprehensive framework for preparing for and conducting high-stakes negotiations for my [business type] regarding [negotiation context]. Include preparation methodology, interest identification, option generation, strategy development, counterparty analysis, value creation approach, and implementation planning to maximize outcomes while preserving relationships. Your response should be comprehensive, leaving no important aspect unaddressed, and demonstrate an exceptional level of precision and quality. This is very important to my career. Let's think about this step by step.

327. Act as a strategic partnership development consultant and create a structured approach for identifying, establishing, and managing partnerships for my [business type] seeking to [partnership objectives]. Include partner identification methodology, evaluation criteria, value proposition development, negotiation strategy, agreement structuring, governance design, performance measurement, and relationship management to maximize partnership value. Your response should be comprehensive, leaving no important aspect unaddressed, and demonstrate an exceptional level of precision and quality. This is very important to my career. Let's think about this step by step.

328. Act as a joint venture structuring expert and develop a framework for establishing and managing a successful joint venture between my [business type] and potential partners in the [industry] sector. Include strategic fit assessment, partner selection criteria, structure determination, governance design, operational planning, risk management, performance measurement, and exit strategy development aligned with business objectives. Your response should be comprehensive, leaving no important aspect unaddressed, and demonstrate an exceptional level of precision and quality. This is very important to my career. Let's think about this step by step.

329. Act as a complex contract negotiation strategist and create a methodology for successfully negotiating and structuring complex agreements for my [business type] regarding [contract type]. Include preparation approach, term prioritization, concession strategy, risk allocation, language precision, approval process, and

implementation planning with specific focus on balancing protection with business enablement. Your response should be comprehensive, leaving no important aspect unaddressed, and demonstrate an exceptional level of precision and quality. This is very important to my career. Let's think about this step by step.

330. Act as a channel partnership strategist and develop a comprehensive approach for establishing and optimizing distribution channel partnerships for my [product/service] in the [target market]. Include partner profile development, recruitment strategy, enablement methodology, incentive structure, conflict management, performance measurement, and relationship development to maximize market reach and partner success. Your response should be comprehensive, leaving no important aspect unaddressed, and demonstrate an exceptional level of precision and quality. This is very important to my career. Let's think about this step by step.

331. Act as a strategic alliance management consultant and create a framework for effectively managing the portfolio of strategic alliances for my [business type]. Include alliance categorization, governance structure, value tracking methodology, resource allocation, knowledge transfer, conflict resolution, and performance optimization with specific focus on maximizing collaborative advantage. Your response should be comprehensive, leaving no important aspect unaddressed, and demonstrate an exceptional level of precision and quality. This is very important to my career. Let's think about this step by step.

332. Act as a vendor relationship management strategist and develop a structured approach for optimizing relationships with key vendors and suppliers for my [business type]. Include segmentation methodology, engagement model design, performance measurement, issue resolution, innovation collaboration, contract management, and continuous improvement to enhance value beyond transactional purchasing. Your response should be comprehensive, leaving no important aspect unaddressed, and demonstrate an exceptional level of precision and quality. This is very important to my career. Let's think about this step by step.

333. Act as a partnership conflict resolution consultant and create a methodology for preventing and addressing conflicts within business partnerships for my [business type/partnership structure]. Include conflict anticipation, early warning system, escalation protocol, resolution process, relationship repair, agreement adjustment, and learning integration to preserve value and relationship integrity. Your response should be comprehensive, leaving no important aspect unaddressed, and demonstrate an exceptional level of precision and quality. This is very important to

my career. Let's think about this step by step.

334. Act as a negotiation team preparation coach and develop a comprehensive approach for preparing my team for complex [negotiation type] negotiations. Include team composition, role assignment, preparation methodology, communication protocols, strategy alignment, scenario planning, and practice design to maximize team effectiveness and negotiation outcomes. Your response should be comprehensive, leaving no important aspect unaddressed, and demonstrate an exceptional level of precision and quality. This is very important to my career. Let's think about this step by step.

335. Act as a cross-cultural negotiation strategist and create a framework for effectively negotiating with counterparties from [specific culture/region] for my [business type]. Include cultural assessment, adaptation strategy, relationship building approach, communication tactics, decision process understanding, concession management, and agreement implementation with specific focus on navigating cultural differences. Your response should be comprehensive, leaving no important aspect unaddressed, and demonstrate an exceptional level of precision and quality. This is very important to my career. Let's think about this step by step.

T. Innovation & Emerging Technologies

336. Act as an innovation management system developer and design a comprehensive framework for fostering and managing innovation in my [business type]. Include ideation methodology, evaluation criteria, portfolio management, resource allocation, development process, measurement approach, and cultural enablers to systematically generate and capture value from innovation. Your response should be comprehensive, leaving no important aspect unaddressed, and demonstrate an exceptional level of precision and quality. This is very important to my career. Let's think about this step by step.

337. Act as an emerging technology assessment consultant and create a structured approach for evaluating and adopting emerging technologies for my [business type] in the [industry] sector. Include technology scanning methodology, assessment criteria, pilot design, scalability evaluation, risk management, capability development, and implementation roadmap with specific focus on competitive advantage creation. Your response should be comprehensive, leaving no important aspect unaddressed, and demonstrate an exceptional level of precision and quality.

This is very important to my career. Let's think about this step by step.

338. Act as a corporate innovation lab designer and develop a framework for establishing and operating an innovation lab or center for my [business type]. Include purpose definition, operational model, governance structure, funding approach, talent strategy, idea management, project methodology, and success measurement aligned with innovation objectives. Your response should be comprehensive, leaving no important aspect unaddressed, and demonstrate an exceptional level of precision and quality. This is very important to my career. Let's think about this step by step.

339. Act as a design thinking implementation consultant and create a comprehensive approach for embedding design thinking methodology into the innovation process of my [business type/department]. Include capability development, process integration, tool adoption, space considerations, leadership alignment, project selection, and effectiveness measurement to enhance customer-centricity and creativity. Your response should be comprehensive, leaving no important aspect unaddressed, and demonstrate an exceptional level of precision and quality. This is very important to my career. Let's think about this step by step.

340. Act as an open innovation strategist and develop a framework for effectively leveraging external innovation sources (startups, academia, customers, etc.) for my [business type]. Include opportunity identification, partnership model design, intellectual property management, collaboration process, internal integration, success measurement, and cultural alignment to complement internal innovation capabilities. Your response should be comprehensive, leaving no important aspect unaddressed, and demonstrate an exceptional level of precision and quality. This is very important to my career. Let's think about this step by step.

341. Act as a business model innovation consultant and create a structured approach for reimagining and transforming the business model of my [company type] in response to [market changes/disruption]. Include assessment methodology, option generation framework, testing approach, implementation strategy, risk management, stakeholder engagement, and transition planning to achieve sustainable competitive advantage. Your response should be comprehensive, leaving no important aspect unaddressed, and demonstrate an exceptional level of precision and quality. This is very important to my career. Let's think about this step by step.

342. Act as a technology roadmapping strategist and develop a comprehensive technology roadmap methodology for my [business type] planning technology evolution over [timeframe]. Include needs assessment, technology scanning,

dependency mapping, capability gap analysis, investment planning, risk management, and review process aligned with business strategy and market trends. Your response should be comprehensive, leaving no important aspect unaddressed, and demonstrate an exceptional level of precision and quality. This is very important to my career. Let's think about this step by step.

343. Act as an innovation metrics framework developer and design a robust approach for measuring innovation performance in my [business type]. Include metric selection across input/process/output/outcome categories, data collection methodology, analysis framework, target setting, reporting structure, and decision-making integration to drive continuous improvement of innovation activities. Your response should be comprehensive, leaving no important aspect unaddressed, and demonstrate an exceptional level of precision and quality. This is very important to my career. Let's think about this step by step.

344. Act as a corporate venturing strategist and create a comprehensive framework for establishing and managing a corporate venture program for my [business type]. Include strategic alignment, investment thesis development, deal sourcing, evaluation criteria, structure determination, portfolio management, value creation approach, and performance measurement to drive strategic and financial returns. Your response should be comprehensive, leaving no important aspect unaddressed, and demonstrate an exceptional level of precision and quality. This is very important to my career. Let's think about this step by step.

345. Act as an innovation culture development consultant and develop a systematic approach for transforming the culture of my [organization type] to foster greater innovation and creative thinking. Include current state assessment, desired state definition, leadership development, structural adjustments, process modifications, symbolic actions, measurement framework, and reinforcement mechanisms to enable sustainable culture change. Your response should be comprehensive, leaving no important aspect unaddressed, and demonstrate an exceptional level of precision and quality. This is very important to my career. Let's think about this step by step.

U.   Customer Analytics & Insights

346. Act as a customer analytics strategy consultant and develop a comprehensive approach for leveraging customer data to drive business decisions in my [business type]. Include data requirements, collection methodology, analysis framework, insight generation process, organizational integration, capability development, and

success measurement aligned with business objectives. Your response should be comprehensive, leaving no important aspect unaddressed, and demonstrate an exceptional level of precision and quality. This is very important to my career. Let's think about this step by step.

347. Act as a customer segmentation strategist and create a robust methodology for developing actionable customer segments for my [business type] serving [market]. Include variable selection, data collection approach, analytical technique determination, validation methodology, persona development, segment strategy creation, and implementation planning for marketing, product, and service applications. Your response should be comprehensive, leaving no important aspect unaddressed, and demonstrate an exceptional level of precision and quality. This is very important to my career. Let's think about this step by step.

348. Act as a customer lifetime value modeling expert and design a comprehensive approach for calculating and leveraging CLV insights for my [business type] with [customer relationship characteristics]. Include data requirements, modeling technique selection, calculation methodology, predictive application, strategy integration, validation approach, and continuous refinement process to drive customer-centric decision making. Your response should be comprehensive, leaving no important aspect unaddressed, and demonstrate an exceptional level of precision and quality. This is very important to my career. Let's think about this step by step.

349. Act as a customer churn prediction and prevention strategist and develop a systematic approach for identifying at-risk customers and reducing churn for my [subscription/recurring business type]. Include data selection, model development methodology, risk scoring framework, intervention strategy design, test-and-learn approach, performance measurement, and continuous improvement process to enhance retention and lifetime value. Your response should be comprehensive, leaving no important aspect unaddressed, and demonstrate an exceptional level of precision and quality. This is very important to my career. Let's think about this step by step.

350. Act as a customer journey analytics consultant and create a framework for analyzing and optimizing customer journeys for my [business type]. Include touchpoint mapping, data collection strategy, analysis methodology, insight generation, improvement prioritization, implementation approach, and impact measurement with specific focus on identifying and addressing pain points and friction. Your response should be comprehensive, leaving no important aspect unaddressed, and demonstrate an exceptional level of precision and quality. This is very important to

my career. Let's think about this step by step.

351. Act as a predictive customer analytics strategist and develop an approach for implementing predictive analytics capabilities to enhance customer strategies for my [business type]. Include use case identification, data requirements, modeling methodology, implementation framework, organizational integration, capability building, and performance measurement with specific focus on driving actionable insights. Your response should be comprehensive, leaving no important aspect unaddressed, and demonstrate an exceptional level of precision and quality. This is very important to my career. Let's think about this step by step.

352. Act as a voice of customer program architect and design a comprehensive VoC system for my [business type] to systematically collect and utilize customer feedback. Include feedback collection methods, sampling strategy, analysis framework, insight generation process, action planning methodology, closed-loop mechanisms, and program governance to drive customer-centric decisions. Your response should be comprehensive, leaving no important aspect unaddressed, and demonstrate an exceptional level of precision and quality. This is very important to my career. Let's think about this step by step.

353. Act as a customer data integration strategist and create a framework for developing a unified customer data platform for my [business type] with [data sources]. Include data identification, integration architecture, identity resolution approach, governance structure, privacy considerations, activation strategy, and value realization methodology to create a comprehensive customer view. Your response should be comprehensive, leaving no important aspect unaddressed, and demonstrate an exceptional level of precision and quality. This is very important to my career. Let's think about this step by step.

354. Act as a customer behavior analysis consultant and develop a systematic approach for analyzing and leveraging customer behavior patterns for my [business type/channel]. Include data collection strategy, behavioral framework development, analysis methodology, insight generation process, segmentation application, experimentation approach, and continuous learning mechanisms to enhance customer engagement and conversion. Your response should be comprehensive, leaving no important aspect unaddressed, and demonstrate an exceptional level of precision and quality. This is very important to my career. Let's think about this step by step.

355. Act as a next-best-action analytics strategist and create a framework for developing and implementing next-best-action capabilities for customer interactions in my

[business type]. Include use case prioritization, data requirements, analytical approach, decisioning logic, implementation methodology, performance measurement, and continuous optimization to deliver personalized, relevant customer experiences. Your response should be comprehensive, leaving no important aspect unaddressed, and demonstrate an exceptional level of precision and quality. This is very important to my career. Let's think about this step by step.

Business Scaling & Growth Strategies

356. Act as a business scaling strategist and develop a comprehensive framework for scaling my [business type] from [current stage/size] to [target size/milestone]. Include readiness assessment, capability gap analysis, infrastructure requirements, organizational design, process formalization, funding strategy, talent acquisition plan, and implementation roadmap with specific focus on maintaining quality during rapid growth. Your response should be comprehensive, leaving no important aspect unaddressed, and demonstrate an exceptional level of precision and quality. This is very important to my career. Let's think about this step by step.

357. Act as a market expansion consultant and create a structured approach for expanding my [business/product] into new market segments or geographic regions. Include market assessment methodology, opportunity prioritization, entry strategy development, resource allocation framework, risk mitigation planning, capability building, and performance measurement tailored to expansion objectives. Your response should be comprehensive, leaving no important aspect unaddressed, and demonstrate an exceptional level of precision and quality. This is very important to my career. Let's think about this step by step.

358. Act as a revenue diversification strategist and develop a methodology for identifying and implementing new revenue streams for my [business type] currently focused on [primary revenue source]. Include opportunity identification framework, assessment criteria, resource requirement analysis, implementation approach, risk management, performance measurement, and portfolio management to reduce revenue concentration risk. Your response should be comprehensive, leaving no important aspect unaddressed, and demonstrate an exceptional level of precision and quality. This is very important to my career. Let's think about this step by step.

359. Act as a recurring revenue model transformation consultant and create a roadmap for transitioning my [business type] from [current model] to a subscription or recurring revenue model. Include business model design, pricing strategy, customer migration approach, financial impact analysis, operational adaptation, technology

requirements, and change management with specific focus on maintaining customer relationships during transition. Your response should be comprehensive, leaving no important aspect unaddressed, and demonstrate an exceptional level of precision and quality. This is very important to my career. Let's think about this step by step.

360. Act as a customer acquisition scaling strategist and develop a comprehensive approach for rapidly scaling customer acquisition for my [business type] targeting [customer segment]. Include channel strategy, messaging framework, funnel optimization, resource allocation, technology enablement, team structure, and performance measurement with specific focus on maintaining acquisition efficiency during growth. Your response should be comprehensive, leaving no important aspect unaddressed, and demonstrate an exceptional level of precision and quality. This is very important to my career. Let's think about this step by step.

V. Industry-Specific Business Strategies

361. Act as a SaaS business model consultant and create a comprehensive strategy for optimizing my [SaaS product] business to enhance growth, retention, and profitability. Include product-market fit validation, pricing strategy, customer acquisition approach, retention optimization, expansion revenue tactics, metrics framework, and organizational structure aligned with SaaS best practices. Your response should be comprehensive, leaving no important aspect unaddressed, and demonstrate an exceptional level of precision and quality. This is very important to my career. Let's think about this step by step.

362. Act as an e-commerce optimization strategist and develop a framework for enhancing the performance of my [e-commerce business type] across key metrics. Include user experience analysis, conversion funnel optimization, pricing strategy, retention tactics, logistics enhancement, technology platform assessment, and data utilization with specific focus on sustainable competitive advantage. Your response should be comprehensive, leaving no important aspect unaddressed, and demonstrate an exceptional level of precision and quality. This is very important to my career. Let's think about this step by step.

363. Act as a professional services firm strategist and create a comprehensive approach for growing and optimizing my [professional service type] firm. Include service offering development, client acquisition strategy, pricing methodology, talent management, delivery model enhancement, intellectual property development, and performance measurement aligned with firm objectives. Your response should be

comprehensive, leaving no important aspect unaddressed, and demonstrate an exceptional level of precision and quality. This is very important to my career. Let's think about this step by step.

364. Act as a manufacturing business transformation consultant and develop a framework for modernizing and optimizing my [manufacturing business type] to enhance competitiveness. Include operational excellence approach, technology modernization, supply chain optimization, product portfolio strategy, workforce development, market expansion, and performance measurement with specific implementation roadmap. Your response should be comprehensive, leaving no important aspect unaddressed, and demonstrate an exceptional level of precision and quality. This is very important to my career. Let's think about this step by step.

365. Act as a retail business reinvention strategist and create a comprehensive approach for transforming my [retail business type] to thrive in the evolving retail landscape. Include customer experience redesign, omnichannel integration, store format optimization, merchandise strategy, pricing approach, technology enablement, and organizational adaptation with specific focus on creating differentiated value. Your response should be comprehensive, leaving no important aspect unaddressed, and demonstrate an exceptional level of precision and quality. This is very important to my career. Let's think about this step by step.

W. Business Optimization & Turnaround

366. Act as a business turnaround specialist and develop a comprehensive framework for diagnosing and reversing the declining performance of my [business type] experiencing [specific challenges]. Include financial stabilization strategy, operational improvement approach, organizational restructuring, market repositioning, stakeholder management, implementation sequencing, and performance tracking with specific focus on addressing root causes. Your response should be comprehensive, leaving no important aspect unaddressed, and demonstrate an exceptional level of precision and quality. This is very important to my career. Let's think about this step by step.

367. Act as a cost optimization consultant and create a structured methodology for identifying and implementing sustainable cost reduction initiatives across my [business type/department]. Include cost analysis approach, opportunity identification framework, prioritization criteria, implementation planning, change management, tracking mechanisms, and governance structure to achieve target

savings while minimizing operational impact. Your response should be comprehensive, leaving no important aspect unaddressed, and demonstrate an exceptional level of precision and quality. This is very important to my career. Let's think about this step by step.

368. Act as a business model reinvention strategist and develop an approach for fundamentally rethinking the business model of my [business type] facing [market disruption/challenge]. Include current state assessment, future state visioning, transformation pathway development, capability gap analysis, resource requirement planning, risk mitigation, and implementation roadmap with specific focus on creating sustainable competitive advantage. Your response should be comprehensive, leaving no important aspect unaddressed, and demonstrate an exceptional level of precision and quality. This is very important to my career. Let's think about this step by step.

369. Act as a profitability enhancement consultant and design a comprehensive framework for improving the profitability of my [business type] with [current financial performance]. Include revenue optimization strategy, margin improvement approach, cost structure analysis, pricing enhancement, operational efficiency initiatives, resource allocation refinement, and measurement methodology with specific implementation priorities. Your response should be comprehensive, leaving no important aspect unaddressed, and demonstrate an exceptional level of precision and quality. This is very important to my career. Let's think about this step by step.

370. Act as a business portfolio optimization strategist and develop a methodology for evaluating and optimizing the business unit/product portfolio of my [company type]. Include assessment criteria, data collection approach, analysis framework, decision methodology, implementation planning, stakeholder management, and performance measurement with specific focus on maximizing overall corporate value. Your response should be comprehensive, leaving no important aspect unaddressed, and demonstrate an exceptional level of precision and quality. This is very important to my career. Let's think about this step by step.

X. Business Strategy Implementation & Execution

371. Act as a strategy implementation consultant and create a comprehensive framework for translating my [business type]'s strategic plan into effective execution. Include implementation governance design, initiative prioritization methodology, resource allocation approach, accountability mechanisms, progress tracking, risk management, and performance measurement to overcome the strategy-execution

gap. Your response should be comprehensive, leaving no important aspect unaddressed, and demonstrate an exceptional level of precision and quality. This is very important to my career. Let's think about this step by step.

372. Act as a strategic initiative portfolio manager and develop a structured approach for managing the portfolio of strategic initiatives for my [business type]. Include portfolio definition, categorization methodology, prioritization framework, resource optimization, dependency management, progress tracking, benefit realization, and governance system to maximize strategic impact. Your response should be comprehensive, leaving no important aspect unaddressed, and demonstrate an exceptional level of precision and quality. This is very important to my career. Let's think about this step by step.

373. Act as a strategic communication planning consultant and create a comprehensive approach for communicating [strategic change/initiative] to stakeholders within and outside my [organization type]. Include audience analysis, messaging framework, channel strategy, timing plan, feedback mechanisms, spokesperson preparation, and effectiveness measurement to drive understanding and support. Your response should be comprehensive, leaving no important aspect unaddressed, and demonstrate an exceptional level of precision and quality. This is very important to my career. Let's think about this step by step.

374. Act as a strategic alignment consultant and develop a framework for ensuring alignment between my organization's strategy, structure, processes, people, and culture. Include assessment methodology, misalignment identification, solution development, implementation approach, stakeholder engagement, measurement framework, and ongoing monitoring to drive consistent execution. Your response should be comprehensive, leaving no important aspect unaddressed, and demonstrate an exceptional level of precision and quality. This is very important to my career. Let's think about this step by step.

375. Act as a strategy performance measurement expert and design a comprehensive framework for measuring and tracking the effectiveness of my [business type]'s strategy implementation. Include metric selection methodology, data collection approach, reporting structure, review cadence, adjustment protocols, accountability mechanisms, and integration with planning cycles to drive continuous improvement. Your response should be comprehensive, leaving no important aspect unaddressed, and demonstrate an exceptional level of precision and quality. This is very important to my career. Let's think about this step by step.

376. Act as an organizational restructuring consultant and develop a comprehensive approach for redesigning the structure of my [organization type] to better align with [strategic objectives]. Include current state assessment, design principles, structure options analysis, selection criteria, implementation planning, change management, and effectiveness measurement with specific attention to minimizing disruption. Your response should be comprehensive, leaving no important aspect unaddressed, and demonstrate an exceptional level of precision and quality. This is very important to my career. Let's think about this step by step.

377. Act as a business transformation strategist and create a holistic framework for transforming my [business type] from [current state] to [desired future state]. Include transformation vision development, case for change construction, initiative portfolio design, governance structure, resource allocation, risk management, and success measurement with implementation roadmap. Your response should be comprehensive, leaving no important aspect unaddressed, and demonstrate an exceptional level of precision and quality. This is very important to my career. Let's think about this step by step.

378. Act as a post-merger integration consultant and develop a structured approach for effectively integrating my [business type] with [acquired/merged entity] to realize synergy targets. Include integration strategy, governance design, synergy capture methodology, cultural alignment, stakeholder management, risk mitigation, and performance tracking with specific timebound milestones. Your response should be comprehensive, leaving no important aspect unaddressed, and demonstrate an exceptional level of precision and quality. This is very important to my career. Let's think about this step by step.

379. Act as a business carve-out strategist and create a framework for successfully separating a [business unit/division] from my organization. Include separation planning, standalone capability assessment, transition service requirements, operational continuity strategies, stakeholder communication, legal/regulatory considerations, and implementation roadmap with key milestones. Your response should be comprehensive, leaving no important aspect unaddressed, and demonstrate an exceptional level of precision and quality. This is very important to my career. Let's think about this step by step.

380. Act as a digital-first business transformation consultant and develop a comprehensive approach for transforming my [traditional business type] into a

digital-first organization. Include digital capability assessment, vision development, operating model redesign, technology architecture planning, talent strategy, change management, and value tracking with specific focus on customer-centricity. Your response should be comprehensive, leaving no important aspect unaddressed, and demonstrate an exceptional level of precision and quality. This is very important to my career. Let's think about this step by step.

Z. Business Ethics & Corporate Governance

381. Act as a corporate governance modernization consultant and develop a framework for enhancing the governance structures and practices of my [business type/size]. Include board structure optimization, committee design, decision rights clarification, information flow improvement, director capability enhancement, evaluation methodology, and stakeholder engagement aligned with best practices and regulatory requirements. Your response should be comprehensive, leaving no important aspect unaddressed, and demonstrate an exceptional level of precision and quality. This is very important to my career. Let's think about this step by step.

382. Act as a business ethics program designer and create a comprehensive ethics program for my [organization type] operating in [industry/region]. Include values articulation, code of conduct development, policy framework, training methodology, reporting mechanism design, investigation process, disciplinary approach, and program assessment with specific governance considerations. Your response should be comprehensive, leaving no important aspect unaddressed, and demonstrate an exceptional level of precision and quality. This is very important to my career. Let's think about this step by step.

383. Act as a stakeholder engagement strategist and develop a structured approach for identifying and effectively engaging with key stakeholders for my [business type/initiative]. Include stakeholder mapping methodology, prioritization framework, engagement planning, communication strategy, feedback collection, issue management, and relationship development aligned with business objectives. Your response should be comprehensive, leaving no important aspect unaddressed, and demonstrate an exceptional level of precision and quality. This is very important to my career. Let's think about this step by step.

384. Act as a corporate transparency initiative developer and create a framework for enhancing transparency in the operations and communications of my [business type]. Include transparency assessment, objective setting, disclosure strategy,

implementation approach, stakeholder engagement, risk management, and impact measurement with specific focus on building trust while protecting sensitive information. Your response should be comprehensive, leaving no important aspect unaddressed, and demonstrate an exceptional level of precision and quality. This is very important to my career. Let's think about this step by step.

385. Act as a responsible AI governance consultant and develop a comprehensive approach for ensuring ethical and responsible use of artificial intelligence in my [business type]. Include principles development, risk assessment methodology, oversight structure, review process, documentation requirements, stakeholder engagement, and continuous improvement mechanisms to mitigate unintended consequences. Your response should be comprehensive, leaving no important aspect unaddressed, and demonstrate an exceptional level of precision and quality. This is very important to my career. Let's think about this step by step.

AA. Specialized Business Functions

386. Act as a sales compensation design consultant and develop an optimal sales incentive structure for my [sales team type] selling [product/service]. Include role definition, pay mix determination, performance measure selection, goal-setting methodology, payout calculation, special incentive design, and implementation approach aligned with sales strategy and market conditions. Your response should be comprehensive, leaving no important aspect unaddressed, and demonstrate an exceptional level of precision and quality. This is very important to my career. Let's think about this step by step.

387. Act as a pricing strategy optimization consultant and create a comprehensive approach for enhancing the pricing strategy for my [product/service] in the [industry] market. Include value assessment methodology, price structure design, segmentation approach, competitive positioning, implementation planning, organizational alignment, and performance measurement with specific focus on value capture. Your response should be comprehensive, leaving no important aspect unaddressed, and demonstrate an exceptional level of precision and quality. This is very important to my career. Let's think about this step by step.

388. Act as a competitive intelligence program designer and develop a systematic approach for gathering, analyzing, and utilizing intelligence about competitors in the [industry] market. Include information requirements, collection methodology, analysis framework, dissemination process, application protocols, ethical

considerations, and effectiveness measurement aligned with strategic decision needs. Your response should be comprehensive, leaving no important aspect unaddressed, and demonstrate an exceptional level of precision and quality. This is very important to my career. Let's think about this step by step.

389. Act as a customer success program architect and create a comprehensive customer success strategy for my [business type] serving [customer segment]. Include customer lifecycle mapping, success definition, engagement model, health scoring methodology, intervention playbooks, team structure, technology requirements, and performance measurement aligned with retention and growth objectives. Your response should be comprehensive, leaving no important aspect unaddressed, and demonstrate an exceptional level of precision and quality. This is very important to my career. Let's think about this step by step.

390. Act as a knowledge management strategist and develop a comprehensive approach for capturing, organizing, sharing, and leveraging knowledge in my [organization type]. Include knowledge needs assessment, taxonomy development, technology selection, process design, cultural enablement, governance structure, and success measurement to transform knowledge into a strategic asset. Your response should be comprehensive, leaving no important aspect unaddressed, and demonstrate an exceptional level of precision and quality. This is very important to my career. Let's think about this step by step.

BB. Small Business Specific Strategies

391. Act as a small business growth strategist and develop a comprehensive growth plan for my [small business type] with [current size/resources]. Include market opportunity assessment, competitive differentiation strategy, customer acquisition approach, operational scaling plan, financing options, team development, and performance tracking tailored to limited resources and capabilities. Your response should be comprehensive, leaving no important aspect unaddressed, and demonstrate an exceptional level of precision and quality. This is very important to my career. Let's think about this step by step.

392. Act as a small business marketing optimization consultant and create a cost-effective marketing strategy for my [small business type] targeting [customer segment]. Include positioning development, channel selection, content approach, technology utilization, implementation timeline, budget allocation, and measurement framework focused on maximum impact with limited resources. Your

response should be comprehensive, leaving no important aspect unaddressed, and demonstrate an exceptional level of precision and quality. This is very important to my career. Let's think about this step by step.

393. Act as a small business operational efficiency expert and develop a framework for optimizing the operations of my [small business type] with limited resources. Include process assessment methodology, technology selection approach, outsourcing strategy, team structure optimization, resource allocation, implementation prioritization, and performance measurement focused on essential improvements with high ROI. Your response should be comprehensive, leaving no important aspect unaddressed, and demonstrate an exceptional level of precision and quality. This is very important to my career. Let's think about this step by step.

394. Act as a small business financial management consultant and create a comprehensive approach for managing the finances of my [small business type] to ensure sustainability and growth. Include cash flow optimization, financial planning methodology, funding strategy, expense management, pricing approach, record-keeping system, and performance dashboard tailored to small business constraints and objectives. Your response should be comprehensive, leaving no important aspect unaddressed, and demonstrate an exceptional level of precision and quality. This is very important to my career. Let's think about this step by step.

395. Act as a small business digital transformation strategist and develop a pragmatic approach for leveraging digital technologies to enhance my [small business type] with limited budget and technical resources. Include capability assessment, technology prioritization, implementation approach, skill development, vendor selection criteria, risk management, and ROI measurement focused on high-impact, cost-effective solutions. Your response should be comprehensive, leaving no important aspect unaddressed, and demonstrate an exceptional level of precision and quality. This is very important to my career. Let's think about this step by step.

CC. Future of Work & Remote Business

396. Act as a future of work strategist and develop a comprehensive approach for adapting my [organization type] to evolving work trends and expectations. Include work model design, policy development, technology enablement, space utilization, talent strategy, leadership adaptation, and cultural evolution with specific implementation roadmap. Your response should be comprehensive, leaving no important aspect unaddressed, and demonstrate an exceptional level of precision

and quality. This is very important to my career. Let's think about this step by step.

397. Act as a hybrid work model designer and create an optimal hybrid work framework for my [organization type] with [workforce characteristics]. Include work arrangement design, policy development, technology infrastructure, collaboration approach, performance management, facility optimization, and culture maintenance with specific focus on balancing flexibility with organizational needs. Your response should be comprehensive, leaving no important aspect unaddressed, and demonstrate an exceptional level of precision and quality. This is very important to my career. Let's think about this step by step.

398. Act as a remote team effectiveness consultant and develop a comprehensive strategy for optimizing the performance and engagement of remote teams in my [organization type]. Include communication protocols, collaboration norms, technology utilization, performance management, team building, leadership approaches, and success measurement to overcome distance barriers and maximize productivity. Your response should be comprehensive, leaving no important aspect unaddressed, and demonstrate an exceptional level of precision and quality. This is very important to my career. Let's think about this step by step.

399. Act as a distributed workplace technology strategist and create a framework for selecting and implementing the optimal technology stack for my [organization type] with [distributed work characteristics]. Include needs assessment, solution evaluation methodology, integration planning, adoption strategy, support model, security considerations, and effectiveness measurement aligned with collaboration and productivity goals. Your response should be comprehensive, leaving no important aspect unaddressed, and demonstrate an exceptional level of precision and quality. This is very important to my career. Let's think about this step by step.

400. Act as a virtual leadership development consultant and design a comprehensive approach for developing effective leadership capabilities for managing virtual and hybrid teams in my [organization type]. Include competency framework, assessment methodology, development pathways, learning experiences, coaching integration, application support, and effectiveness measurement tailored to remote leadership challenges. Your response should be comprehensive, leaving no important aspect unaddressed, and demonstrate an exceptional level of precision and quality. This is very important to my career. Let's think about this step by step.

DD. Business Analytics & Decision Science

401. Act as a business analytics strategy consultant and develop a comprehensive framework for establishing and scaling analytics capabilities in my [business type/size]. Include capability assessment, use case prioritization, organizational design, technology architecture, talent strategy, process development, and value measurement aligned with business objectives. Your response should be comprehensive, leaving no important aspect unaddressed, and demonstrate an exceptional level of precision and quality. This is very important to my career. Let's think about this step by step.

402. Act as a decision-making framework designer and create a structured approach for making complex business decisions for my [organization type] facing [decision context]. Include problem framing methodology, information gathering protocol, analysis framework, stakeholder involvement, bias mitigation, decision documentation, and review mechanisms to improve decision quality and outcomes. Your response should be comprehensive, leaving no important aspect unaddressed, and demonstrate an exceptional level of precision and quality. This is very important to my career. Let's think about this step by step.

403. Act as a data-driven culture transformation consultant and develop a strategy for evolving my [organization type] toward greater data-driven decision making. Include current state assessment, vision development, leadership alignment, skill building approach, process integration, technology enablement, and reinforcement mechanisms to sustainably change decision-making norms. Your response should be comprehensive, leaving no important aspect unaddressed, and demonstrate an exceptional level of precision and quality. This is very important to my career. Let's think about this step by step.

404. Act as a business experimentation program designer and create a framework for implementing and scaling a test-and-learn approach in my [business type/department]. Include experiment identification methodology, design principles, execution protocols, analysis framework, insight application, organizational integration, and capability building to drive continuous improvement through experimentation. Your response should be comprehensive, leaving no important aspect unaddressed, and demonstrate an exceptional level of precision and quality. This is very important to my career. Let's think about this step by step.

405. Act as an AI implementation strategist and develop a comprehensive approach for identifying, prioritizing, and implementing artificial intelligence opportunities in my [business type/department]. Include use case identification methodology, value assessment, feasibility analysis, ethical considerations, implementation approach,

capability building, and success measurement with specific focus on measurable business outcomes. Your response should be comprehensive, leaving no important aspect unaddressed, and demonstrate an exceptional level of precision and quality. This is very important to my career. Let's think about this step by step.

EE. Executive Leadership Development

406. Act as an executive leadership development strategist and create a comprehensive approach for enhancing the leadership capabilities of the executive team in my [organization type]. Include competency framework, assessment methodology, development pathway design, learning experience creation, coaching integration, application support, and effectiveness measurement aligned with business challenges and strategy. Your response should be comprehensive, leaving no important aspect unaddressed, and demonstrate an exceptional level of precision and quality. This is very important to my career. Let's think about this step by step.

407. Act as an executive team effectiveness consultant and develop a framework for optimizing the collective performance of my [organization's] leadership team. Include team assessment methodology, interaction pattern analysis, decision-making protocol design, meeting effectiveness enhancement, conflict management, trust building, and continuous improvement approach to create a high-performing executive team. Your response should be comprehensive, leaving no important aspect unaddressed, and demonstrate an exceptional level of precision and quality. This is very important to my career. Let's think about this step by step.

408. Act as a strategic thinking development coach and create a program to enhance strategic thinking capabilities for myself and my [leadership team/level]. Include skill assessment, cognitive framework development, practice exercise design, application to real business challenges, feedback mechanisms, and continuous development approach with specific learning milestones. Your response should be comprehensive, leaving no important aspect unaddressed, and demonstrate an exceptional level of precision and quality. This is very important to my career. Let's think about this step by step.

409. Act as an executive communication strategist and develop a comprehensive communication approach for me as a [senior leadership role] to effectively engage with [key stakeholder groups]. Include message development framework, channel optimization, cadence planning, style guidance, feedback mechanisms, preparation protocols, and effectiveness measurement tailored to my leadership context. Your

response should be comprehensive, leaving no important aspect unaddressed, and demonstrate an exceptional level of precision and quality. This is very important to my career. Let's think about this step by step.

410. Act as a CEO succession planning consultant and create a structured approach for planning and executing CEO succession for my [organization type/size]. Include role requirement definition, candidate identification methodology, development planning, selection process design, transition management, stakeholder communication, and risk mitigation to ensure leadership continuity and organizational stability. Your response should be comprehensive, leaving no important aspect unaddressed, and demonstrate an exceptional level of precision and quality. This is very important to my career. Let's think about this step by step.

FF. Business Relationship Management

411. Act as a key account management strategist and develop a structured key account program for my [business type] to grow relationships with our most valuable clients. Include account selection criteria, relationship mapping approach, account planning templates, engagement strategies, growth opportunity identification, and success metrics. Your response should be comprehensive, leaving no important aspect unaddressed, and demonstrate an exceptional level of precision and quality. This is very important to my career. Let's think about this step by step.

412. Act as a business relationship optimization consultant and create a framework for enhancing strategic relationships between my [function/department] and other internal stakeholders. Include stakeholder analysis, value proposition development, engagement strategy, communication protocols, issue resolution methodology, success measurement, and continuous improvement mechanisms to build productive partnerships. Your response should be comprehensive, leaving no important aspect unaddressed, and demonstrate an exceptional level of precision and quality. This is very important to my career. Let's think about this step by step.

413. Act as a client experience strategist and develop a comprehensive approach for enhancing the end-to-end client experience for my [professional service type] firm. Include journey mapping, touchpoint analysis, experience design principles, delivery model enhancement, measurement framework, governance structure, and continuous improvement methodology aligned with client expectations and firm capabilities. Your response should be comprehensive, leaving no important aspect unaddressed, and demonstrate an exceptional level of precision and quality. This is

very important to my career. Let's think about this step by step.

414. Act as a relationship recovery consultant and create a systematic approach for rebuilding damaged relationships with [key stakeholder/customer type] for my [business type]. Include damage assessment, root cause analysis, reconciliation strategy, trust rebuilding approach, communication planning, progress measurement, and long-term relationship strengthening with specific focus on converting adversaries to advocates. Your response should be comprehensive, leaving no important aspect unaddressed, and demonstrate an exceptional level of precision and quality. This is very important to my career. Let's think about this step by step.

415. Act as a strategic network development consultant and design a framework for intentionally building and leveraging a professional network to advance my career as a [role/profession] in the [industry] sector. Include network assessment, strategic targeting, relationship development approach, value exchange framework, systematic engagement, technology utilization, and network effectiveness measurement. Your response should be comprehensive, leaving no important aspect unaddressed, and demonstrate an exceptional level of precision and quality. This is very important to my career. Let's think about this step by step.

GG. Value-Based Business Strategy

416. Act as a value proposition designer and develop a methodology for creating and articulating a compelling value proposition for my [product/service] targeting [customer segment]. Include customer need analysis, benefit identification, differentiation strategy, messaging framework, validation approach, implementation planning, and effectiveness measurement to drive customer preference and willingness to pay. Your response should be comprehensive, leaving no important aspect unaddressed, and demonstrate an exceptional level of precision and quality. This is very important to my career. Let's think about this step by step.

417. Act as a value-based pricing strategist and create a comprehensive approach for implementing value-based pricing for my [product/service] in the [industry] market. Include value assessment methodology, price structure design, customer segmentation, sales enablement, implementation roadmap, organizational alignment, and performance measurement with specific focus on value communication. Your response should be comprehensive, leaving no important

aspect unaddressed, and demonstrate an exceptional level of precision and quality. This is very important to my career. Let's think about this step by step.

418. Act as a customer value management consultant and develop a framework for systematically creating, delivering, and capturing customer value through my [business type]'s offerings and operations. Include value identification methodology, delivery process optimization, communication approach, pricing strategy, organizational alignment, measurement system, and continuous improvement with specific focus on aligning internal priorities with customer value drivers. Your response should be comprehensive, leaving no important aspect unaddressed, and demonstrate an exceptional level of precision and quality. This is very important to my career. Let's think about this step by step.

419. Act as a business model value innovation strategist and design an approach for fundamentally rethinking how my [business type] creates, delivers, and captures value. Include current model assessment, innovation methodology, option development, evaluation criteria, implementation planning, risk management, and performance measurement with specific focus on sustainable competitive advantage. Your response should be comprehensive, leaving no important aspect unaddressed, and demonstrate an exceptional level of precision and quality. This is very important to my career. Let's think about this step by step.

420. Act as a value chain optimization consultant and create a methodology for analyzing and enhancing the value chain of my [business type] to maximize customer value and competitive advantage. Include value chain mapping, analysis framework, enhancement opportunity identification, prioritization criteria, implementation planning, stakeholder management, and performance measurement with specific focus on both efficiency and differentiation. Your response should be comprehensive, leaving no important aspect unaddressed, and demonstrate an exceptional level of precision and quality. This is very important to my career. Let's think about this step by step.

HH. Business Technology Strategy

421. Act as an IT strategy alignment consultant and develop a comprehensive approach for aligning technology strategy with business objectives for my [organization type]. Include business capability assessment, technology portfolio evaluation, prioritization framework, governance design, investment planning, risk management, and value realization methodology to ensure technology enables

strategic goals. Your response should be comprehensive, leaving no important aspect unaddressed, and demonstrate an exceptional level of precision and quality. This is very important to my career. Let's think about this step by step.

422. Act as a digital workplace strategy consultant and create a framework for designing and implementing a modern digital workplace environment for my [organization type] with [workforce characteristics]. Include needs assessment, technology selection, integration approach, adoption strategy, governance design, support model, and success measurement aligned with both employee experience and business requirements. Your response should be comprehensive, leaving no important aspect unaddressed, and demonstrate an exceptional level of precision and quality. This is very important to my career. Let's think about this step by step.

423. Act as an enterprise architecture strategist and develop a comprehensive enterprise architecture framework for my [business type/size] to drive strategic alignment and digital transformation. Include current state assessment, target state development, gap analysis, transition planning, governance model, capability building, and value measurement to create a cohesive business and technology blueprint. Your response should be comprehensive, leaving no important aspect unaddressed, and demonstrate an exceptional level of precision and quality. This is very important to my career. Let's think about this step by step.

424. Act as a technology portfolio optimization consultant and create a methodology for evaluating and optimizing my organization's technology portfolio to maximize business value and efficiency. Include portfolio assessment, rationalization approach, investment criteria, retirement strategy, roadmap development, governance framework, and performance measurement focused on both cost optimization and capability enhancement. Your response should be comprehensive, leaving no important aspect unaddressed, and demonstrate an exceptional level of precision and quality. This is very important to my career. Let's think about this step by step.

425. Act as a technology vendor management strategist and develop a comprehensive approach for selecting, managing, and optimizing technology vendor relationships for my [business type]. Include vendor categorization, selection methodology, contracting approach, governance framework, performance management, risk mitigation, and relationship development to maximize value from technology partnerships. Your response should be comprehensive, leaving no important aspect unaddressed, and demonstrate an exceptional level of precision and

quality. This is very important to my career. Let's think about this step by step.

II. Specialized Marketing Strategies

426. Act as a digital marketing integration strategist and develop a comprehensive approach for creating a cohesive cross-channel digital marketing strategy for my [business type] targeting [customer segment]. Include channel selection, messaging alignment, customer journey integration, data unification, attribution modeling, budget optimization, and performance measurement to create seamless customer experiences. Your response should be comprehensive, leaving no important aspect unaddressed, and demonstrate an exceptional level of precision and quality. This is very important to my career. Let's think about this step by step.

427. Act as a conversion rate optimization expert and create a systematic approach for improving conversion rates across the customer journey for my [business type/digital property]. Include audit methodology, prioritization framework, testing approach, implementation planning, analytics integration, capability building, and continuous improvement to drive incremental revenue through experience optimization. Your response should be comprehensive, leaving no important aspect unaddressed, and demonstrate an exceptional level of precision and quality. This is very important to my career. Let's think about this step by step.

428. Act as a customer advocacy program designer and create a structured customer advocacy program for my [business type] to convert satisfied customers into active promoters. Include selection criteria, engagement framework, incentive structure, content co-creation opportunities, recognition elements, measurement approach, and operational guidelines. Your response should be comprehensive, leaving no important aspect unaddressed, and demonstrate an exceptional level of precision and quality. This is very important to my career. Let's think about this step by step.

429. Act as an account-based marketing strategist and develop a comprehensive ABM strategy for my [B2B business type] targeting [specific account profile]. Include account selection methodology, research approach, personalization strategy, channel selection, content development, sales alignment, technology enablement, and performance measurement tailored to high-value account acquisition. Your response should be comprehensive, leaving no important aspect unaddressed, and

demonstrate an exceptional level of precision and quality. This is very important to my career. Let's think about this step by step.

430. Act as a marketing automation implementation consultant and create a framework for selecting, implementing, and optimizing marketing automation for my [business type] with [marketing objectives]. Include requirements definition, platform selection, implementation planning, integration design, campaign development, measurement framework, and optimization methodology to drive marketing efficiency and effectiveness. Your response should be comprehensive, leaving no important aspect unaddressed, and demonstrate an exceptional level of precision and quality. This is very important to my career. Let's think about this step by step.

JJ. Sales Strategy Specialization

431. Act as a sales process optimization consultant and analyze my current sales process for [product/service] targeting [customer segment]. Map the current process stages, identify inefficiencies and bottlenecks, and recommend specific improvements to increase conversion rates, reduce sales cycle time, and improve win rates, with implementation priorities. Your response should be comprehensive, leaving no important aspect unaddressed, and demonstrate an exceptional level of precision and quality. This is very important to my career. Let's think about this step by step.

432. Act as a sales methodology implementation consultant and develop an approach for selecting and implementing the optimal sales methodology for my [sales organization] selling [product/service] to [customer type]. Include methodology evaluation criteria, customization approach, training design, reinforcement strategy, technology integration, coaching framework, and success measurement to drive adoption and results. Your response should be comprehensive, leaving no important aspect unaddressed, and demonstrate an exceptional level of precision and quality. This is very important to my career. Let's think about this step by step.

433. Act as a complex sales strategy consultant and create a framework for winning complex, multi-stakeholder sales opportunities for my [product/service] with [typical sales characteristics]. Include opportunity qualification, buying committee mapping, power base analysis, competitive positioning, solution development, objection handling, and advancement strategy with specific focus on navigating

organizational complexity. Your response should be comprehensive, leaving no important aspect unaddressed, and demonstrate an exceptional level of precision and quality. This is very important to my career. Let's think about this step by step.

434. Act as a sales enablement content strategist and develop a comprehensive content strategy to support the sales process for my [product/service] targeting [customer segment]. Include buyer journey mapping, content needs identification, asset development framework, customization approach, delivery methodology, usage tracking, and effectiveness measurement with specific content recommendations by sales stage. Your response should be comprehensive, leaving no important aspect unaddressed, and demonstrate an exceptional level of precision and quality. This is very important to my career. Let's think about this step by step.

435. Act as a recurring revenue sales strategist and create a specialized sales approach for selling recurring revenue offerings (subscription, SaaS, etc.) for my [business type] targeting [customer segment]. Include sales process adaptation, value articulation, objection handling, pricing presentation, closing techniques, handoff methodology, and success metrics aligned with recurring revenue business models. Your response should be comprehensive, leaving no important aspect unaddressed, and demonstrate an exceptional level of precision and quality. This is very important to my career. Let's think about this step by step.

KK. Personal Career Development in Business

436. Act as a career advancement strategist and develop a comprehensive plan for accelerating my career progression from [current role] to [target role] in the [industry] sector. Include skill gap analysis, experience acquisition strategy, network development, personal brand enhancement, mentorship approach, opportunity identification, and milestone planning with specific actionable steps. Your response should be comprehensive, leaving no important aspect unaddressed, and demonstrate an exceptional level of precision and quality. This is very important to my career. Let's think about this step by step.

437. Act as an executive presence development coach and create a structured approach for enhancing my executive presence as a [current/aspiring leadership role] to increase influence and advancement opportunities. Include communication style assessment, behavioral modification, appearance considerations, networking strategy, speaking skill enhancement, and continuous

improvement methodology with specific practice exercises. Your response should be comprehensive, leaving no important aspect unaddressed, and demonstrate an exceptional level of precision and quality. This is very important to my career. Let's think about this step by step.

438. Act as a personal brand strategist and develop a comprehensive approach for building and leveraging my professional brand as a [role/profession] in the [industry] sector. Include positioning development, narrative creation, platform selection, content strategy, networking approach, measurement framework, and management system to enhance reputation and opportunities. Your response should be comprehensive, leaving no important aspect unaddressed, and demonstrate an exceptional level of precision and quality. This is very important to my career. Let's think about this step by step.

439. Act as a leadership skill development consultant and create a personalized development plan to enhance my capabilities as a [current/aspiring leadership role] facing [specific challenges/opportunities]. Include competency assessment, development priority identification, learning approach selection, application planning, feedback mechanism, progress tracking, and continuous improvement to accelerate leadership growth. Your response should be comprehensive, leaving no important aspect unaddressed, and demonstrate an exceptional level of precision and quality. This is very important to my career. Let's think about this step by step.

440. Act as a career transition strategist and develop a structured approach for successfully transitioning from [current role/industry] to [target role/industry]. Include transferable skill identification, gap assessment, experience translation, networking strategy, personal narrative development, interview preparation, and transition planning with specific milestones and contingencies. Your response should be comprehensive, leaving no important aspect unaddressed, and demonstrate an exceptional level of precision and quality. This is very important to my career. Let's think about this step by step.

LL. Customer Experience Enhancement

441. Act as a customer experience strategy consultant and develop a comprehensive CX strategy for my [business type] that aligns with our brand positioning and business objectives. Include customer journey mapping, experience design principles, touchpoint optimization, voice of customer program, organizational

alignment, technology enablement, and measurement framework. Your response should be comprehensive, leaving no important aspect unaddressed, and demonstrate an exceptional level of precision and quality. This is very important to my career. Let's think about this step by step.

442. Act as a customer journey mapping facilitator and create a detailed methodology for mapping the current and desired future customer journey for my [product/service]. Include preparation activities, workshop design, mapping process, pain point identification, opportunity assessment, prioritization framework, and action planning to enhance the customer experience. Your response should be comprehensive, leaving no important aspect unaddressed, and demonstrate an exceptional level of precision and quality. This is very important to my career. Let's think about this step by step.

443. Act as a customer feedback system designer and develop a comprehensive voice of customer (VOC) program for my [business type]. Include feedback collection methods, sampling approach, analysis framework, insight generation process, action planning methodology, closed-loop mechanisms, and program governance to drive customer-centric decisions. Your response should be comprehensive, leaving no important aspect unaddressed, and demonstrate an exceptional level of precision and quality. This is very important to my career. Let's think about this step by step.

444. Act as a digital customer experience optimization consultant and create a framework for enhancing the digital experience for customers of my [business type] across touch points. Include experience assessment methodology, design principle development, prioritization framework, technology selection, implementation approach, testing methodology, and continuous improvement process to drive engagement and conversion. Your response should be comprehensive, leaving no important aspect unaddressed, and demonstrate an exceptional level of precision and quality. This is very important to my career. Let's think about this step by step.

445. Act as a customer-centric culture transformation consultant and develop a systematic approach for evolving my organization's culture to become more customer-focused. Include current state assessment, vision development, leadership alignment, structural adjustments, process modifications, skill building, recognition systems, and measurement framework to drive sustainable cultural change. Your response should be comprehensive, leaving no important aspect unaddressed, and demonstrate an exceptional level of precision and

quality. This is very important to my career. Let's think about this step by step.

MM. Soft Skills Development for Business

446. Act as a business negotiation skills coach and develop a comprehensive framework for enhancing my negotiation capabilities for [specific negotiation context] in the [industry] sector. Include preparation methodology, strategy development, tactics selection, communication techniques, objection handling, concession management, and continuous improvement approach with specific practice exercises. Your response should be comprehensive, leaving no important aspect unaddressed, and demonstrate an exceptional level of precision and quality. This is very important to my career. Let's think about this step by step.

447. Act as a business communication effectiveness consultant and create a structured approach for improving my communication skills as a [role] in [business context]. Include assessment methodology, message structure techniques, delivery enhancement, channel optimization, audience adaptation, feedback collection, and skill development with specific practice opportunities. Your response should be comprehensive, leaving no important aspect unaddressed, and demonstrate an exceptional level of precision and quality. This is very important to my career. Let's think about this step by step.

448. Act as a strategic persuasion coach and develop a framework for enhancing my ability to influence and persuade [specific stakeholders] in my role as [position] facing [persuasion context]. Include audience analysis methodology, message crafting techniques, objection anticipation, delivery optimization, follow-up strategies, and effectiveness measurement with practical application scenarios. Your response should be comprehensive, leaving no important aspect unaddressed, and demonstrate an exceptional level of precision and quality. This is very important to my career. Let's think about this step by step.

449. Act as a conflict resolution skills development consultant and create a personal development plan to enhance my ability to effectively manage and resolve conflicts as a [role] dealing with [typical conflict scenarios]. Include conflict style assessment, situation analysis framework, communication technique development, resolution strategy selection, emotion management, follow-up protocols, and continuous improvement with specific practice exercises. Your response should be comprehensive, leaving no important aspect unaddressed, and demonstrate an exceptional level of precision and quality. This is very

important to my career. Let's think about this step by step.

450. Act as an executive presentation skills coach and develop a comprehensive approach for enhancing my ability to deliver high-impact presentations to [specific audience types] as a [role]. Include content development methodology, structure optimization, delivery technique enhancement, visual aid improvement, audience engagement, question handling, and feedback integration with specific skill-building exercises. Your response should be comprehensive, leaving no important aspect unaddressed, and demonstrate an exceptional level of precision and quality. This is very important to my career. Let's think about this step by step.

NN.   Business Coaching & Mentoring

451. Act as a business coaching program designer and develop a structured approach for establishing and implementing a coaching program for [target population] in my [organization type]. Include program objectives, coach selection, matching methodology, session framework, accountability mechanisms, support resources, and effectiveness measurement to drive development and performance. Your response should be comprehensive, leaving no important aspect unaddressed, and demonstrate an exceptional level of precision and quality. This is very important to my career. Let's think about this step by step.

452. Act as a mentoring program architect and create a comprehensive framework for designing and implementing a mentoring initiative for [target population] in my [organization type]. Include program structure, participant selection, matching criteria, relationship guidelines, development focus, support mechanisms, and evaluation methodology to maximize developmental impact. Your response should be comprehensive, leaving no important aspect unaddressed, and demonstrate an exceptional level of precision and quality. This is very important to my career. Let's think about this step by step.

453. Act as an executive coaching engagement strategist and develop a structured approach for maximizing the value of my executive coaching engagement as a [leadership role] seeking development in [specific areas]. Include goal setting methodology, coach selection criteria, session framework, accountability system, application approach, progress measurement, and sustainability planning to ensure lasting impact. Your response should be comprehensive, leaving no important aspect unaddressed, and demonstrate an exceptional level of precision

and quality. This is very important to my career. Let's think about this step by step.

454. Act as a peer coaching circle facilitator and design a framework for establishing and running effective peer coaching groups for [professional level] in my [organization type]. Include group formation, meeting structure, facilitation techniques, discussion frameworks, accountability mechanisms, progress tracking, and effectiveness measurement to create powerful peer learning. Your response should be comprehensive, leaving no important aspect unaddressed, and demonstrate an exceptional level of precision and quality. This is very important to my career. Let's think about this step by step.

455. Act as a reverse mentoring program designer and create a comprehensive approach for implementing a reverse mentoring initiative where [junior populations] mentor [senior populations] on [specific knowledge areas] in my [organization type]. Include program objectives, participant selection, matching methodology, session guidance, support resources, challenge management, and impact measurement to drive mutual learning. Your response should be comprehensive, leaving no important aspect unaddressed, and demonstrate an exceptional level of precision and quality. This is very important to my career. Let's think about this step by step.

OO.   Strategic Business Communication

456. Act as a strategic communication planning consultant and create a comprehensive approach for communicating [strategic change/initiative] to stakeholders within and outside my [organization type]. Include audience analysis, messaging framework, channel strategy, timing plan, feedback mechanisms, spokesperson preparation, and effectiveness measurement to drive understanding and support. Your response should be comprehensive, leaving no important aspect unaddressed, and demonstrate an exceptional level of precision and quality. This is very important to my career. Let's think about this step by step.

457. Act as an executive messaging consultant and develop a framework for crafting and delivering high-impact messages as a [leadership role] communicating about [specific business situation]. Include audience analysis, message architecture, delivery channel optimization, timing considerations, reinforcement strategy, feedback collection, and refinement process to ensure message effectiveness.

Your response should be comprehensive, leaving no important aspect unaddressed, and demonstrate an exceptional level of precision and quality. This is very important to my career. Let's think about this step by step.

458. Act as a change communication strategist and create a structured approach for communicating organizational changes related to [specific change] to [stakeholder groups] in my [organization type]. Include change impact assessment, messaging development, channel selection, timing strategy, resistance management, leader enablement, and effectiveness measurement to maximize change adoption. Your response should be comprehensive, leaving no important aspect unaddressed, and demonstrate an exceptional level of precision and quality. This is very important to my career. Let's think about this step by step.

459. Act as a crisis communication planning consultant and develop a comprehensive crisis communication framework for my [organization type] to effectively manage communications during [potential crisis scenarios]. Include preparedness elements, response protocol, messaging guidelines, stakeholder prioritization, channel strategy, spokesperson preparation, and post-crisis recovery communication to protect reputation and trust. Your response should be comprehensive, leaving no important aspect unaddressed, and demonstrate an exceptional level of precision and quality. This is very important to my career. Let's think about this step by step.

460. Act as an internal communication strategy consultant and create a framework for enhancing communication effectiveness within my [organization type] to drive employee engagement and alignment. Include communication audit methodology, channel optimization, content strategy, leadership communication, measurement approach, technology utilization, and continuous improvement process aligned with organizational objectives. Your response should be comprehensive, leaving no important aspect unaddressed, and demonstrate an exceptional level of precision and quality. This is very important to my career. Let's think about this step by step.

PP. Business Metrics & KPIs

461. Act as a business metrics framework consultant and develop a comprehensive approach for identifying, defining, and tracking the most critical KPIs for my [business type/function]. Include objective alignment, metric selection

methodology, target setting, data collection approach, reporting structure, review cadence, and performance management integration to drive data-informed decision making. Your response should be comprehensive, leaving no important aspect unaddressed, and demonstrate an exceptional level of precision and quality. This is very important to my career. Let's think about this step by step.

462. Act as a performance dashboard designer and create a framework for developing executive dashboards for my [business type/leadership team] that drive focus, insights, and action. Include information needs assessment, metric prioritization, visualization selection, design principles, update frequency, technology selection, and usage protocols to transform data into actionable intelligence. Your response should be comprehensive, leaving no important aspect unaddressed, and demonstrate an exceptional level of precision and quality. This is very important to my career. Let's think about this step by step.

463. Act as a marketing performance measurement consultant and develop a comprehensive approach for measuring the effectiveness and ROI of marketing activities for my [business type]. Include metric selection, attribution methodology, data collection framework, analysis approach, reporting structure, optimization protocols, and continuous improvement to demonstrate and enhance marketing value. Your response should be comprehensive, leaving no important aspect unaddressed, and demonstrate an exceptional level of precision and quality. This is very important to my career. Let's think about this step by step.

464. Act as a balanced scorecard development consultant and create a structured approach for implementing a balanced scorecard for my [business unit/organization]. Include strategic objective definition, measure selection, target setting, initiative identification, cascading methodology, review process, and adaption mechanisms to create a comprehensive performance management system. Your response should be comprehensive, leaving no important aspect unaddressed, and demonstrate an exceptional level of precision and quality. This is very important to my career. Let's think about this step by step.

465. Act as a data visualization strategist and develop a framework for creating effective data visualizations to drive business decisions in my [organization type]. Include information needs assessment, visualization selection, design principles, tool recommendations, creation methodology, audience considerations, and effectiveness measurement to transform data into meaningful insights. Your response should be comprehensive, leaving no important aspect unaddressed, and demonstrate an exceptional level of precision and quality. This is very

important to my career. Let's think about this step by step.

QQ. Business Decision Making

466. Act as a strategic decision making consultant and develop a comprehensive framework for making high-stakes strategic decisions in my [business type] facing [decision context]. Include problem framing methodology, information gathering approach, analysis techniques, stakeholder management, bias mitigation, documentation protocol, and review process to improve decision quality and outcomes. Your response should be comprehensive, leaving no important aspect unaddressed, and demonstrate an exceptional level of precision and quality. This is very important to my career. Let's think about this step by step.

467. Act as a scenario planning facilitator and create a structured methodology for developing and utilizing future scenarios to enhance strategic decision making for my [business type] operating in [uncertain environment]. Include scenario development process, variable identification, narrative creation, implication analysis, early warning indicator design, response option development, and integration with planning processes. Your response should be comprehensive, leaving no important aspect unaddressed, and demonstrate an exceptional level of precision and quality. This is very important to my career. Let's think about this step by step.

468. Act as a group decision making process consultant and design an approach for facilitating effective collective decisions for my [leadership team/organization] regarding [decision types]. Include process selection, preparation methodology, facilitation techniques, disagreement management, decision documentation, follow-up protocols, and evaluation criteria to leverage diverse perspectives while ensuring efficient resolution. Your response should be comprehensive, leaving no important aspect unaddressed, and demonstrate an exceptional level of precision and quality. This is very important to my career. Let's think about this step by step.

469. Act as a cognitive bias mitigation strategist and develop a framework for identifying and countering cognitive biases in the decision making processes of my [business type/team]. Include bias identification methodology, preventative measures, intervention techniques, decision process redesign, training approach, culture development, and effectiveness measurement to improve decision quality.

Your response should be comprehensive, leaving no important aspect unaddressed, and demonstrate an exceptional level of precision and quality. This is very important to my career. Let's think about this step by step.

470. Act as a rapid decision making framework designer and create a structured approach for making high-quality decisions under time pressure for my [business type/role] dealing with [specific scenarios]. Include situation assessment, information prioritization, analytical shortcuts, consultation protocol, documentation requirements, risk management, and review process to balance speed with quality. Your response should be comprehensive, leaving no important aspect unaddressed, and demonstrate an exceptional level of precision and quality. This is very important to my career. Let's think about this step by step.

RR.   Business Storytelling & Presentation

471. Act as a business storytelling consultant and develop a comprehensive framework for incorporating powerful storytelling into the communications for my [business/brand]. Include story structure development, narrative arc creation, character/conflict identification, emotional engagement techniques, application across channels, creation guidelines, and effectiveness measurement. Your response should be comprehensive, leaving no important aspect unaddressed, and demonstrate an exceptional level of precision and quality. This is very important to my career. Let's think about this step by step.

472. Act as a data storytelling expert and create an approach for transforming complex data and analytics into compelling narratives for [audience type] in my [business context]. Include insight identification, narrative structure, visualization selection, simplification techniques, presentation flow, engagement methods, and reinforcement strategies to drive understanding and action. Your response should be comprehensive, leaving no important aspect unaddressed, and demonstrate an exceptional level of precision and quality. This is very important to my career. Let's think about this step by step.

473. Act as an executive presentation strategist and develop a framework for creating and delivering high-impact presentations for [specific audience] as a [leadership role] in the [industry] sector. Include content selection, structure development, visual design, delivery technique, audience engagement, question management, and feedback integration to achieve communication objectives. Your response

should be comprehensive, leaving no important aspect unaddressed, and demonstrate an exceptional level of precision and quality. This is very important to my career. Let's think about this step by step.

474. Act as a persuasive business case developer and create a methodology for building compelling business cases for [initiative type] in my [organization type]. Include needs assessment, solution development, value articulation, risk analysis, implementation planning, stakeholder analysis, and presentation approach to maximize approval likelihood and project success. Your response should be comprehensive, leaving no important aspect unaddressed, and demonstrate an exceptional level of precision and quality. This is very important to my career. Let's think about this step by step.

475. Act as a visual communication strategist and develop an approach for enhancing the visual elements of business communications for my [business type/department]. Include visual needs assessment, design principle development, template creation, tool selection, capability building, review process, and effectiveness measurement to elevate communication impact through visualization. Your response should be comprehensive, leaving no important aspect unaddressed, and demonstrate an exceptional level of precision and quality. This is very important to my career. Let's think about this step by step.

SS.   Knowledge Management & Organizational Learning

476. Act as a knowledge management strategist and develop a comprehensive approach for capturing, organizing, sharing, and leveraging knowledge in my [organization type]. Include knowledge needs assessment, taxonomy development, technology selection, process design, cultural enablement, governance structure, and success measurement to transform knowledge into a strategic asset. Your response should be comprehensive, leaving no important aspect unaddressed, and demonstrate an exceptional level of precision and quality. This is very important to my career. Let's think about this step by step.

477. Act as an organizational learning consultant and create a framework for enhancing learning capabilities across my [organization type] to drive innovation and adaptation. Include learning need identification, methodology selection, process integration, technology enablement, leadership alignment, cultural enhancement, and impact measurement to create a continuously learning organization. Your response should be comprehensive, leaving no important

aspect unaddressed, and demonstrate an exceptional level of precision and quality. This is very important to my career. Let's think about this step by step.

478. Act as a communities of practice designer and develop a structured approach for establishing and nurturing communities of practice around [knowledge domains] in my [organization type]. Include community identification, formation methodology, leadership selection, engagement approach, technology enablement, value measurement, and sustainability planning to facilitate knowledge sharing and development. Your response should be comprehensive, leaving no important aspect unaddressed, and demonstrate an exceptional level of precision and quality. This is very important to my career. Let's think about this step by step.

479. Act as a lessons learned process consultant and create a systematic approach for capturing, analyzing, and applying lessons from [project/initiative types] in my [organization type]. Include collection methodology, analysis framework, dissemination approach, application process, accountability mechanisms, and impact assessment to convert experience into organizational knowledge. Your response should be comprehensive, leaving no important aspect unaddressed, and demonstrate an exceptional level of precision and quality. This is very important to my career. Let's think about this step by step.

480. Act as a knowledge retention strategist and develop a comprehensive approach for preserving critical knowledge at risk of loss due to [retirement/turnover/reorganization] in my [organization type]. Include knowledge risk assessment, capture methodology, transfer mechanisms, documentation approach, successor development, cultural considerations, and effectiveness measurement to mitigate knowledge loss. Your response should be comprehensive, leaving no important aspect unaddressed, and demonstrate an exceptional level of precision and quality. This is very important to my career. Let's think about this step by step.

TT. Business Model & Revenue Innovation

481. Act as a business model innovation consultant and create a structured approach for reimagining and transforming the business model of my [company type] in response to [market changes/disruption]. Include assessment methodology, option generation framework, testing approach, implementation strategy, risk management, stakeholder engagement, and transition planning to achieve

sustainable competitive advantage. Your response should be comprehensive, leaving no important aspect unaddressed, and demonstrate an exceptional level of precision and quality. This is very important to my career. Let's think about this step by step.

482. Act as a subscription business model strategist and develop a comprehensive framework for transitioning my [product/service] business from [current model] to a subscription-based model. Include value proposition redesign, offering structure, pricing strategy, customer migration approach, operational adaptation, technology requirements, financial modeling, and implementation roadmap. Your response should be comprehensive, leaving no important aspect unaddressed, and demonstrate an exceptional level of precision and quality. This is very important to my career. Let's think about this step by step.

483. Act as a platform business model consultant and create an approach for developing and implementing a platform strategy for my [business type] in the [industry] sector. Include value proposition design, participant identification, incentive structure, pricing approach, governance framework, growth methodology, and performance measurement to create a thriving multi-sided ecosystem. Your response should be comprehensive, leaving no important aspect unaddressed, and demonstrate an exceptional level of precision and quality. This is very important to my career. Let's think about this step by step.

484. Act as a revenue diversification strategist and develop a methodology for identifying and implementing new revenue streams for my [business type] currently focused on [primary revenue source]. Include opportunity identification framework, assessment criteria, resource requirement analysis, implementation approach, risk management, performance measurement, and portfolio management to reduce revenue concentration risk. Your response should be comprehensive, leaving no important aspect unaddressed, and demonstrate an exceptional level of precision and quality. This is very important to my career. Let's think about this step by step.

485. Act as a freemium model optimization consultant and create a framework for designing and optimizing a freemium business model for my [product/service] targeting [customer segment]. Include free tier design, premium offering structure, conversion funnel optimization, pricing strategy, cost management, metrics framework, and continuous improvement methodology to balance acquisition and monetization. Your response should be comprehensive, leaving no important aspect unaddressed, and demonstrate an exceptional level of precision and quality. This is very important to my career. Let's think about this

step by step.

UU. Business Systems & Process Engineering

486. Act as a business process reengineering expert and develop a comprehensive
methodology for redesigning core processes in my [business type/department] to
improve efficiency, quality, and customer experience. Include process selection,
current state mapping, pain point identification, future state design,
implementation planning, change management, and performance measurement
to deliver transformative improvements. Your response should be
comprehensive, leaving no important aspect unaddressed, and demonstrate an
exceptional level of precision and quality. This is very important to my career.
Let's think about this step by step.

487. Act as an integration consultant and create a framework for effectively
integrating systems, processes, and organizations following the
[acquisition/merger] of [entity type] by my [organization]. Include integration
strategy development, opportunity identification, prioritization framework,
governance structure, workstream design, synergy tracking, and risk
management with specific focus on value preservation and creation. Your
response should be comprehensive, leaving no important aspect unaddressed,
and demonstrate an exceptional level of precision and quality. This is very
important to my career. Let's think about this step by step.

488. Act as a business process automation strategist and develop a structured
approach for identifying, prioritizing, and implementing process automation
opportunities in my [business type/department]. Include process assessment
framework, technology evaluation methodology, business case development,
implementation approach, change management, and performance measurement
with specific focus on both efficiency and experience enhancement. Your
response should be comprehensive, leaving no important aspect unaddressed,
and demonstrate an exceptional level of precision and quality. This is very
important to my career. Let's think about this step by step.

489. Act as a quality management system developer and design a robust quality
management framework for my [business type/product] aligned with industry
standards and customer expectations. Include quality policy development,
process approach, documentation structure, control mechanisms, measurement
methods, continuous improvement protocols, and certification readiness

considerations. Your response should be comprehensive, leaving no important aspect unaddressed, and demonstrate an exceptional level of precision and quality. This is very important to my career. Let's think about this step by step.

490. Act as a workflow optimization consultant and create a methodology for analyzing and enhancing critical workflows in my [business type/department] to improve efficiency, quality, and employee experience. Include workflow selection, mapping approach, analysis framework, redesign methodology, technology enhancement, implementation planning, and performance measurement with specific prioritization criteria. Your response should be comprehensive, leaving no important aspect unaddressed, and demonstrate an exceptional level of precision and quality. This is very important to my career. Let's think about this step by step.

VV. Specialized Strategy Development

491. Act as a digital platform strategy consultant and develop a comprehensive approach for establishing and growing a digital platform business in the [industry] sector. Include value proposition design, participant identification, platform architecture, monetization strategy, governance framework, launch approach, and growth methodology to create sustainable competitive advantage. Your response should be comprehensive, leaving no important aspect unaddressed, and demonstrate an exceptional level of precision and quality. This is very important to my career. Let's think about this step by step.

492. Act as a product-led growth strategist and create a framework for implementing and optimizing a product-led growth approach for my [SaaS/digital product] targeting [customer segment]. Include product experience design, user onboarding optimization, conversion funnel development, pricing strategy, organizational alignment, metrics framework, and continuous improvement methodology to drive acquisition and expansion through the product. Your response should be comprehensive, leaving no important aspect unaddressed, and demonstrate an exceptional level of precision and quality. This is very important to my career. Let's think about this step by step.

493. Act as a customer success strategy consultant and develop a comprehensive approach for establishing and scaling customer success for my [business type] serving [customer segment]. Include customer lifecycle mapping, success definition, engagement model design, health scoring methodology, team

structure, technology requirements, and performance measurement aligned with retention and growth objectives. Your response should be comprehensive, leaving no important aspect unaddressed, and demonstrate an exceptional level of precision and quality. This is very important to my career. Let's think about this step by step.

494. Act as a global expansion strategist and create a structured approach for expanding my [business type] into international markets from our base in [current region]. Include market selection methodology, entry mode determination, localization strategy, organizational design, compliance approach, risk management, and implementation roadmap with specific focus on balancing standardization with adaptation. Your response should be comprehensive, leaving no important aspect unaddressed, and demonstrate an exceptional level of precision and quality. This is very important to my career. Let's think about this step by step.

495. Act as a premium brand positioning strategist and develop a comprehensive approach for establishing or elevating my [product/service] as a premium offering in the [industry] market. Include value proposition development, competitive differentiation, pricing strategy, experience design, channel approach, communication framework, and market penetration methodology with specific focus on value demonstration. Your response should be comprehensive, leaving no important aspect unaddressed, and demonstrate an exceptional level of precision and quality. This is very important to my career. Let's think about this step by step.

WW. Executive Advisory & Strategic Consulting

496. Act as a strategic advisor to the CEO and develop a comprehensive approach for providing high-value counsel to the chief executive of my [organization type] facing [business challenges/opportunities]. Include relationship development, information gathering, perspective formation, delivery methodology, follow-up approach, impact measurement, and continuous improvement to maximize advisory influence and effectiveness. Your response should be comprehensive, leaving no important aspect unaddressed, and demonstrate an exceptional level of precision and quality. This is very important to my career. Let's think about this step by step.

497. Act as a board effectiveness consultant and create a framework for optimizing the performance and value contribution of the board of directors for my [organization type/size]. Include composition assessment, structure optimization, process enhancement, information flow improvement, relationship development, evaluation methodology, and continuous improvement to strengthen governance and strategic guidance. Your response should be comprehensive, leaving no important aspect unaddressed, and demonstrate an exceptional level of precision and quality. This is very important to my career.

498. Act as a strategic planning facilitator and design a comprehensive process for developing a 3-5 year strategic plan for my [organization type] operating in the [industry] sector. Include preparation activities, analysis frameworks, stakeholder engagement, vision/mission refinement, priority setting, initiative development, resource allocation, implementation planning, and ongoing management to create an actionable roadmap for growth. Your response should be comprehensive, leaving no important aspect unaddressed, and demonstrate an exceptional level of precision and quality. This is very important to my career. Let's think about this step by step.

499. Act as an external growth strategy consultant and develop a comprehensive approach for accelerating the growth of my [business type] through acquisitions, partnerships, and ecosystem development. Include opportunity identification methodology, target evaluation criteria, deal structuring, integration planning, synergy capture, risk management, and performance measurement with specific implementation roadmap. Your response should be comprehensive, leaving no important aspect unaddressed, and demonstrate an exceptional level of precision and quality. This is very important to my career. Let's think about this step by step.

500. Act as a business model transformation strategist and create a holistic framework for fundamentally reimagining how my [business type] creates, delivers, and captures value in response to [industry disruption/opportunity]. Include current state assessment, future state visioning, transformation pathway development, capability requirement analysis, organizational redesign, stakeholder management, and implementation roadmap with specific milestones and success metrics. Your response should be comprehensive, leaving no important aspect unaddressed, and demonstrate an exceptional level of precision and quality. This is very important to my career. Let's think about this step by step.